Quick Scripture Reference for Counseling Couples

Quick Scripture Reference for Counseling Couples

KEITH R. MILLER *and*
PATRICIA A. MILLER

BakerBooks
a division of Baker Publishing Group
Grand Rapids, Michigan

Published by Baker Books
a division of Baker Publishing Group
P.O. Box 6287, Grand Rapids, MI 49516-6287
www.bakerbooks.com

Printed in the United States of America

Library of Congress Cataloging-in-Publication Data
Names: Miller, Keith R., author.
Title: Quick scripture reference for counseling couples / Keith R. Miller and Patricia A. Miller.
Description: Grand Rapids : Baker Books, 2016.
Identifiers: LCCN 2016039061 | ISBN 9780801019043 (spiral)
Subjects: LCSH: Marriage—Biblical teaching. | Marriage counseling.
Classification: LCC BS680.M35 M55 2016 | DDC 206/.1—dc23
LC record available at https://lccn.loc.gov/2016039061

17 18 19 20 21 22 23 7 6 5 4 3 2 1

In keeping with biblical principles of creation stewardship, Baker Publishing Group advocates the responsible use of our natural resources. As a member of the Green Press Initiative, our company uses recycled paper when possible. The text paper of this book is composed in part of post-consumer waste.

To all our students at Calvary Bible College.
You have impacted our lives more
than you will ever know.

Contents

Subject Guide

Acknowledgments

A special thank you to Baker Publishing Group and especially Chad Allen for the honor of requesting that we proceed with this fourth book in our Quick Scripture Reference for Counseling series.

Our great desire is that God's Word will do its saving and healing work for all who use this book.

To God be the glory!

Introduction

The Purpose of This Book

This book is grounded on the sufficiency of the Word of God for faith and practice, for living the life that God desires, and for direction and counseling. It is written for men and women who are anticipating marriage or who are married and dealing with the issues of life together and for counselors and pastors who minister to couples. Topics have been chosen that are specific to those needs.

Context and Principles

We have made every effort to be true to context. For those texts for which the context does not totally fit, we believe the principles (timeless, universal truths) do apply to the topic being discussed. Many of the Old Testament passages refer, in context, to Israel. Yet the principles reflecting God's care for his people and interest in their welfare can clearly be seen.

The use of passages from the Mosaic Law reflects our conviction that the traditional moral, civil, and ceremonial distinctions for that code are correct. God's moral law, as summarized in the Ten Commandments, is applicable for all people, for all time. Though the civil and ceremonial laws are not our rule of life in this age of grace, they do reflect the mind of God on issues of right and wrong, good and bad. Thus principles are drawn from them for the topics.

What to Look For

- There are two divisions: Part One—Preparing for Marriage is for couples who are engaged (or considering the commitment). Part Two—Living in Marriage is for those who have already entered into marriage and need to understand biblical truth regarding the ongoing events of the relationship.
- There are two avenues for locating desired topics: 1) a "Contents" section, with headings and topics grouped beneath, and 2) a separate "Subject Guide," with all topics listed alphabetically.
- The gospel is the first topic. It is necessary for everyone to be in a personal relationship with Jesus Christ as Savior and committed to him as Lord of their lives. It is essential to evaluate this issue before any counseling problems are addressed. God's Word is useful in anyone's life, but when believers use the Word, the Holy Spirit has power in their lives to help them truly understand Scripture and make necessary changes. Biblical counseling can then be effective.
- The "See also" heading at the beginning of each topic points to related helpful topics.
- Many of the topics begin with a paragraph of introduction that defines key words and concepts, setting the stage for what follows in the body of statements and supporting Scripture.
- The section "Practical Steps" provides homework growth projects or action ideas. Use them as a starting point to stimulate your own creativity for additional steps.
- The "Resources" section at the end of each topic is a guide to books and booklets helpful for further research and understanding. There is a wide range of authors and publishers, and each resource was chosen with care, but we would not necessarily agree with every statement contained in each book.
- To avoid constant repetition of biblical texts, some of the topics provide cross-references to other related topics.
- Because of space and copyright limitations, some of the verses are not printed, with many additional references listed for further study and application.

Who Might Benefit

- First and foremost this book is designed to assist counselors, pastors, and anyone who desires to help men and women in the struggles, issues, and joys of married life.
- Men and women who desire to live their lives together under the authority and blessing of God's Word can use this book for personal study and application of the various topics.
- This book can be used as a devotional. These topics could be a tool used each day for a man or woman's time alone with the Lord. Taking two days for reading and study of each topic would provide over six months of concerted involvement in Scripture. The couple could discuss the topics together.
- Those who teach in the local church concerning marriage could use the various topics as teaching or supporting material. Similar topics could be grouped together to cover a thirteen-week quarter.
- Bible studies for groups, men, women, or couples could also find helpful material in this book.

The Gospel

The gospel is the place where our relationship with God begins.

A counselor's first task is to determine if the person or couple has a personal relationship with Jesus Christ. Help can still be provided for the problems and struggles they face, but it is only when someone understands and applies the gospel personally that Scripture will make sense.

When a person has trusted Jesus Christ and him alone for salvation, Scripture, with the power of the Holy Spirit, will then truly be able to do its work.

Steps in Guiding an Individual to Christ

If possible, have counselees read the passages from a Bible.

1. **Each person is separated from God because of sin and sinful behavior.**

   Romans 3:23 For all have sinned and fall short of the glory of God. (NKJV)

   Isaiah 53:6 All we like sheep have gone astray; we have turned, every one, to his own way; and the Lord has laid on Him the iniquity of us all. (NKJV)

2. **Sin must be punished—that punishment is separation from God, in hell.**

   Romans 6:23 For the wages of sin is death, but the gift of God is eternal life in Christ Jesus our Lord. (NKJV)

3. **There is nothing a person can do to gain status with God or to work for their salvation. We cannot earn forgiveness.**

 Ephesians 2:8–9 For by grace you have been saved through faith. And this is not your own doing; it is the gift of God, not a result of works, so that no one may boast. (ESV)

 Titus 3:5 He saved us, not because of works done by us in righteousness, but according to his own mercy, by the washing of regeneration and renewal of the Holy Spirit. (ESV)

 Isaiah 64:6 We have all become like one who is unclean, and all our righteous deeds are like a polluted garment. We all fade like a leaf, and our iniquities, like the wind, take us away. (ESV)

4. **God recognizes this dilemma. From creation he put a plan into action to give individuals the opportunity to have a personal relationship with him. This plan was based on the death of his Son, Jesus Christ.**

 Romans 5:8 But God demonstrates His own love toward us, in that while we were still sinners, Christ died for us. (NKJV)

 John 3:16 For God so loved the world that He gave His only begotten Son, that whoever believes in Him should not perish but have everlasting life. (NKJV)

 Romans 10:9 Because, if you confess with your mouth that Jesus is Lord and believe in your heart that God raised him from the dead, you will be saved. (ESV)

5. **Each person must repent of their sin and personally believe (i.e., trust) in Jesus Christ as the only way to receive God's forgiveness and gain entrance into heaven.**

 John 1:12 But as many as received Him, to them He gave the right to become children of God, even to those who believe in His name. (NASB)

 John 3:36 Whoever believes in the Son has eternal life, but whoever rejects the Son will not see life, for God's wrath remains on them. (NIV)

 Luke 15:7, 10 In the same way, there is more joy in heaven over one lost sinner who repents and returns to God than over ninety-nine others who are righteous and haven't strayed away! . . . In the same way, there is joy in the presence of God's angels when even one sinner repents. (NLT)

6. **Salvation is then assured—not a "maybe" or "hope so"; it is God's gift.**

   1 John 5:13 I write these things to you who believe in the name of the Son of God that you may know that you have eternal life. (ESV)

   John 5:24 Truly, truly, I say to you, whoever hears my word and believes him who sent me has eternal life. He does not come into judgment, but has passed from death to life. (ESV)

7. **Biblical examples/pictures of salvation:**

   Nicodemus, **John 3**
   Serpent in the wilderness, **Numbers 21 with John 3:14**
   Woman at the well, **John 4**
   Ethiopian, **Acts 8**
   Cornelius, **Acts 10**
   Philippian jailor, **Acts 16**

Practical Steps

- For the best model/illustration of what the gospel looks like, do a comparison study of the serpent in the wilderness (Numbers 21:4–9) with John 3:14.
- Study carefully the Gospel of John. Note the multiple times "believe" is used.
- Write out your spiritual journey. Compare it to each area listed in this topic. Do you have an accurate picture according to Scripture?
- Question to ask: "If you were to die soon, why would you expect God to allow you to join him in heaven?"

Resources

- *Assurance* (booklet). Susan Heck. Focus.
- *Crazy Love: Overwhelmed by a Relentless God*. Francis Chan. David Cook.
- *A Gospel Primer for Christians*. Milton Vincent. Focus.
- *The Jesus I Never Knew*. Philip Yancey. Zondervan.
- *The Reason for God*. Timothy Keller. Dutton.
- *What's So Amazing About Grace?*. Philip Yancey. Zondervan.

Part One

Preparing for Marriage

You're engaged! You have chosen that one person out of all others with whom you want to spend the rest of your life. You believe that God has brought you together. Plans are being made. For the best planning of all, you need to know the basics from God's Word about understanding and preparing for your lives together!

Marriage in the Beginning

See also **Cohabitation, Contentment, Roles in Marriage, Waiting for Sex**

1. **From the very beginning, marriage was a part of God's creative plan and design.**

   Genesis 2:18–24 And the Lord God said, "It is not good that man should be alone; I will make him a helper comparable to him." . . . And the Lord God caused a deep sleep to fall on Adam, and he slept; and He took one of his ribs, and closed up the flesh in its place. Then the rib which the Lord God had taken from man He made into a woman, and He brought her to the man. And Adam said: "This is now bone of my bones and flesh of my flesh; she shall be called Woman, because she was taken out of Man." Therefore a man shall leave his father and mother and be joined to his wife, and they shall become one flesh. (NKJV)

   Genesis 1:27; Matthew 19:4–6

2. **Marriage is honorable and for life. God's design is for marriage to last.**

   Mark 10:7–9 For this reason a man shall leave his father and mother and be joined to his wife, and the two shall become one flesh; so then they are no longer two, but one flesh. Therefore what God has joined together, let not man separate. (NKJV)

   Malachi 2:14 You ask, "Why?" It is because the Lord is the witness between you and the wife of your youth. You have been unfaithful to her, though she is your partner, the wife of your marriage covenant. (NIV)

   Hebrews 13:4 Let marriage be held in honor among all, and let the marriage bed be undefiled, for God will judge the sexually immoral and adulterous. (ESV)

   1 Corinthians 7:39

3. **Sexual intimacy must be reserved for marriage.**

   Proverbs 5:15–18 Drink water from your own cistern, running water from your own well. Should your springs overflow in the streets, your streams of water in the public squares? Let them be yours alone, never to be shared with strangers. May your fountain be blessed, and may you rejoice in the wife of your youth. (NIV)

   1 Corinthians 7:2 But since sexual immorality is occurring, each man should have sexual relations with his own wife, and each woman with her own husband. (NIV)

4. **From the beginning, marriage was to be between only a man and a woman. There is no same-sex marriage in God's plan.**

   Genesis 1:27 God created man in His own image, in the image of God He created him; male and female He created them. (NASB)

   Genesis 2:20–25 For Adam there was not found a helper suitable for him. So the Lord God caused a deep sleep to fall upon the man, and he slept; then He took one of his ribs and closed up the flesh at that place. The Lord God fashioned into a woman the rib which He had taken from the man, and brought her to the man. The man said, "This is now bone of my bones, and flesh of my flesh; she shall be called Woman, because she was taken out of Man." For this reason a man shall leave his father and his mother, and be joined to his wife; and they shall become one flesh. And the man and his wife were both naked and were not ashamed. (NASB)

   Romans 1:24–27 Therefore God gave them over in the lusts of their hearts to impurity, so that their bodies would be dishonored among them. For they exchanged the truth of God for a lie, and worshiped and served the creature rather than the Creator, who is blessed forever. Amen. For this reason God gave them over to degrading passions; for their women exchanged the natural function for that which is unnatural, and in the same way also the men abandoned the natural function of the woman and burned in their desire toward one another, men with men committing indecent acts and receiving in their own persons the due penalty of their error. (NASB)

Leviticus 20:13 If there is a man who lies with a male as those who lie with a woman, both of them have committed a detestable act. (NASB)

Galatians 5:19–21

Practical Steps

- Begin to pray with each other on a regular basis.
- As a couple, take time to write down your goals for how you want your coming wedding and marriage to honor God.
- Make sure you are working on communication. This aspect of your relationship won't get any easier once you are married. Don't allow conflicts to build.
- Take time to read to each other out loud. Use Scripture, and choose books on building your relationship. Begin with *The Meaning of Marriage* by Tim and Kathy Keller; discuss the material.

Resources

- *Designed for Joy: How the Gospel Impacts Men and Women, Identity and Practice*. Jonathan Parnell and Owen Strachan. Crossway.
- *God, Marriage and Family*. Andreas Kostenberger. Crossway.
- *Love, Sex, and Lasting Relationships*. Chip Ingram. Baker.
- *The Meaning of Marriage*. Timothy and Kathy Keller. Hodder & Stoughton.
- *Preparing for Marriage God's Way*. Wayne Mack. P&R.
- *What Did You Expect? Redeeming the Realities of Marriage*. Paul Tripp. Crossway.

Fearfully and Wonderfully Made

See also **Materialism, Pride, Roles in Marriage, Self-Worth**

As a couple prepares to enter into the marriage relationship, it is helpful to understand the purpose and dignity of life, that God has a plan and design for human beings above all his creation.

1. **Men and women are the crown of creation, awesomely fashioned. God makes a strong statement of satisfaction after his culminating effort during creation's sixth day.**

   Genesis 1:27, 31 So God created mankind. . . . God saw all that he had made, and it was very good. And there was evening, and there was morning—the sixth day. (NIV)

   Psalm 139:13–14 For you created my inmost being; you knit me together in my mother's womb. I praise you because I am fearfully and wonderfully made; your works are wonderful, I know that full well. (NIV)

   Genesis 1:26–31; 2:7, 18–22

2. **Men and women are of equal value in God's sight. Both are created in God's image. Believers are one in Christ Jesus.**

   Genesis 1:27 So God created mankind in his own image, in the image of God he created them; male and female he created them. (NIV)

   Galatians 3:28 There is neither male nor female; for you are all one in Christ Jesus. (NASB)

3. **Our purpose for living begins and ends with bringing glory to God.**

    Psalm 115:1 Not to us, O LORD, not to us, but to your name give glory, for the sake of your steadfast love and your faithfulness! (ESV)

    Isaiah 43:7 Bring all who claim me as their God, for I have made them for my glory. It was I who created them. (NLT)

    2 Corinthians 5:9 So whether we are here in this body or away from this body, our goal is to please him. (NLT)

    1 Corinthians 10:31 So, whether you eat or drink, or whatever you do, do all to the glory of God. (ESV)

    1 Chronicles 16:24–29; Psalm 127:1; Ephesians 2:10; Colossians 3:23

Practical Steps

- Complete a thorough study of the Genesis 1 and Galatians 3 passages that teach the co–image bearer concept.
- As a couple, write out your life goals. Make sure they are Scripture-based, centered on bringing glory to God.
- Spend time discussing each of your hopes, dreams, and ambitions.
- At the end of each day, evaluate how you were able to bring glory to God and what you can improve.

Resources

- *Designed for Joy: How the Gospel Impacts Men and Women, Identity and Practice*. Jonathan Parnell and Owen Strachan. Crossway.
- *Fearfully and Wonderfully Made*. Philip Yancey and Paul Brand. Zondervan.
- "Sexuality" in *Culture Shock*. Chip Ingram. Baker.

Choosing the Right Person

See also **Decision Making**

One question we often hear from our college students is, "How did you know that your wife/husband was the right one for you?" Most of them have great anticipation about being married, yet are unsure about how best to make that choice and get it right. Key issues include knowing the will of God, and keeping Christ at the center of one's life. Also, avoid being in a rush; remember the carpenter's dictum—measure twice, cut once!

1. **Believers must marry believers. God's Word is clear. Israel's failure to do this in the Old Testament provides an example of what to avoid.**

   2 Corinthians 6:14–15 Don't team up with those who are unbelievers. How can righteousness be a partner with wickedness? How can light live with darkness? What harmony can there be between Christ and the devil? (NLT)

   Judges 3:6–7 They took their daughters for themselves as wives, and gave their own daughters to their sons, and served their gods. The sons of Israel did what was evil in the sight of the LORD, and forgot the LORD their God and served the Baals and the Asheroth. (NASB)

   Genesis 24:1–4; Nehemiah 13:26–27

2. **Pray continually and earnestly for God's leading to the right person.**

   Psalm 25:4–5 Teach me your ways, O LORD; make them known to me. Teach me to live according to your truth, for you are my God, who saves me. I always trust in you. (GNT)

James 1:5 But if any of you lack wisdom, you should pray to God, who will give it to you; because God gives generously and graciously to all. (GNT)

James 3:17 But the wisdom from above is pure first of all; it is also peaceful, gentle, and friendly; it is full of compassion and produces a harvest of good deeds; it is free from prejudice and hypocrisy. (GNT)

Jeremiah 10:23; 1 Thessalonians 5:16–19

3. **Make sure your heart is submissive and desires to do God's will. He will provide direction.**

Psalm 40:8 How I love to do your will, my God! I keep your teaching in my heart. (GNT)

Psalm 25:12–14 Who, then, are those who fear the Lord? He will instruct them in the ways they should choose. They will spend their days in prosperity, and their descendants will inherit the land. The Lord confides in those who fear him; he makes his covenant known to them. (NIV)

Psalm 48:14 For this God is our God for ever and ever; he will be our guide even to the end. (NIV)

Proverbs 3:5–6; 4:11–13; Isaiah 42:16

4. **Seek counsel from strong Christians who evidence wisdom and maturity. Their prayers are significant.**

Proverbs 11:14 Without wise leadership, a nation falls; there is safety in having many advisers. (NLT)

Proverbs 15:22 Plans go wrong for lack of advice; many advisers bring success. (NLT)

Colossians 1:9–10 So we have not stopped praying for you since we first heard about you. We ask God to give you complete knowledge of his will and to give you spiritual wisdom and understanding. Then the way you live will always honor and please the Lord, and your lives will produce every kind of good fruit. (NLT)

5. **Support from parents is important; include them in this decision. Seek their advice.**

Ephesians 6:2–3 Honor your father and mother (which is the first commandment with a promise), so that it may be well with you, and that you may live long on the earth. (NASB)

Proverbs 4:20–23 My son, give attention to my words; incline your ear to my sayings. Do not let them depart from your sight; keep them in the midst of your heart. For they are life to those who find them and health to all their body. Watch over your heart with all diligence, for from it flow the springs of life. (NASB)

Proverbs 5:1–2; 6:20–22

6. **Being satisfied with Christ and making him the focus of your life is a priority.**

Psalm 37:4 Delight yourself in the Lord, and he will give you the desires of your heart. (ESV)

Matthew 6:33 Seek the Kingdom of God above all else, and live righteously, and he will give you everything you need. (NLT)

Psalm 145:15–19

7. **Rushing into marriage is never wise.**

Proverbs 19:2 Desire without knowledge is not good—how much more will hasty feet miss the way! (NIV)

Isaiah 33:2 O Lord, be gracious to us; we have waited for You. Be their strength every morning, our salvation also in the time of distress. (NASB)

Isaiah 40:31 They who wait for the Lord shall renew their strength; they shall mount up with wings like eagles; they shall run and not be weary; they shall walk and not faint. (ESV)

Psalm 37:7 Be still before the Lord and wait patiently for him. (ESV)

Practical Steps

- Avoid serious dating with nonbelievers. This is a trap that could easily cause grief. And don't be thinking, "I'll win him or her to the Lord." That could happen, but it's usually not the case.
- Get others praying for you as you approach this all-important decision of choosing the one you will marry.
- Spend time with future in-laws to observe how they treat each other. This could be an indicator of how your future spouse will treat you.

Resources

- *Passion and Purity: Learning to Bring Your Love-Life under Christ's Control*. Elisabeth Elliot. Revell.
- *Pre-Engagement: Five Questions to Ask Yourselves* (booklet). David Powlison. P&R.
- *Preparing for Marriage*. Dennis Rainey, ed. Bethany House.
- *Preparing for Marriage God's Way*. Wayne Mack. P&R.
- *Should We Get Married?* (booklet). William Smith. New Growth.

Handling the Past

See also **Abuse, Anxiety, Confession, Forgiveness from God, Forgiving Each Other, Grief, Trusting God**

One or both of you may bring baggage from the past to this marriage. You might have hurt and pain from harsh treatment or you may have experienced hardship that was beyond your control. Past sins could also be a factor and may affect this relationship. Each individual needs to handle these situations biblically in his or her own life. You may also wonder how your spouse will respond to this information. It is important to know and apply God's Word concerning the past as you enter into marriage.

1. **A constant rehashing of past accomplishments, failures, and losses can trap us into negative thinking that limits our ability to be successful in the present or future.**

 Ezra 3:11–13 And all the people shouted with a great shout when they praised the Lord, because the foundation of the house of the Lord was laid. But many of the priests and Levites and heads of fathers' houses, old men who had seen the first house, wept with a loud voice when they saw the foundation of this house being laid, though many shouted aloud for joy, so that the people could not distinguish the sound of the joyful shout from the sound of the people's weeping. (ESV) (See context for the story in Haggai 1–2.)

 Psalm 13:2 How long must I wrestle with my thoughts and day after day have sorrow in my heart? How long will my enemy triumph over me? (NIV)

 Psalm 42:3–5 Day and night I cry, and tears are my only food; all the time my enemies ask me, "Where is your God?" My heart breaks when I remember the past, when I went with the crowds to the house of God and led them as they walked along, a happy crowd, singing and shouting praise to God. Why am I so sad? Why am I so troubled? I will put my hope in God, and once again I will praise him, my savior and my God. (GNT)

2. **Our need is to remember all God has done for us and his provision in the past. Will he not do the same now?**

Deuteronomy 8:2 And you shall remember the whole way that the LORD your God has led you these forty years in the wilderness. (ESV) (The context of this passage is a test for obedience, but the principle still applies.)

Psalm 143:5–6 I remember the days of old; I meditate on all that you have done; I ponder the work of your hands. I stretch out my hands to you; my soul thirsts for you like a parched land. (ESV)

Joshua 21:45 Not one word of all the good promises that the LORD had made to the house of Israel had failed; all came to pass. (ESV)

Psalm 34:4 I sought the LORD, and he answered me and delivered me from all my fears. (ESV)

Isaiah 43:18–19 Remember not the former things, nor consider the things of old. Behold, I am doing a new thing; now it springs forth, do you not perceive it? I will make a way in the wilderness and rivers in the desert. (ESV)

Philippians 3:13–14 Brothers, I do not consider that I have made it my own. But one thing I do: forgetting what lies behind and straining forward to what lies ahead, I press on toward the goal for the prize of the upward call of God in Christ Jesus. (ESV)

Psalm 77:11; Philippians 4:8

3. **If our past involves sin, and repentance and confession have happened, the need is to focus on the fact of God's forgiveness. Openness and honesty with your spouse are important.**

1 John 1:9 If we confess our sins, He is faithful and righteous to forgive us our sins and to cleanse us from all unrighteousness. (NASB)

Micah 7:18–19 Who is a God like You, who pardons iniquity and passes over the rebellious act of the remnant of his possession? He does not retain His anger forever, because He delights in unchanging love. He will again have compassion on us; He will tread our iniquities under foot. Yes, You will cast all their sins into the depths of the sea. (NASB)

Psalm 25:6–7 Remember your mercy, O Lord, and your steadfast love, for they have been from of old. Remember not the sins of my youth or my transgressions; according to your steadfast love remember me, for the sake of your goodness, O Lord! (ESV)

2 Corinthians 5:17 Therefore, if anyone is in Christ, he is a new creation. The old has passed away; behold, the new has come. (ESV)

4. **There is no sin so great that God will not forgive.**

Psalm 86:5 For you, O Lord, are good and forgiving, abounding in steadfast love to all who call upon you. (ESV)

Daniel 9:9 The Lord our God is merciful and forgiving, even though we have rebelled against him. (NIV)

Psalm 130:3–4; Lamentations 3:22

5. **God will supply complete restoration.**

Colossians 1:13–14 For he has rescued us from the kingdom of darkness and transferred us into the Kingdom of his dear Son, who purchased our freedom and forgave our sins. (NLT)

Romans 8:1–2 There is therefore now no condemnation for those who are in Christ Jesus. For the law of the Spirit of life has set you free in Christ Jesus from the law of sin and death. (ESV)

Psalm 130:7 Put your hope in the Lord, for with the Lord is unfailing love and with him is full redemption. (NIV)

Psalm 51; Psalm 103:10–11

6. **Focus on what God is doing right now and will do in the future.**

Philippians 4:8 Finally, brothers, whatever is true, whatever is honorable, whatever is just, whatever is pure, whatever is lovely, whatever is commendable, if there is any excellence, if there is anything worthy of praise, think about these things. (ESV)

Practical Steps

- If you discuss past indiscretions with each other, don't feel that you have to reveal every detail. Often, a general openness will suffice.
- When you forgive, it means you no longer hold it to the other person's account. Do not nag, remind, or bring up these matters again. Forgive as you have been forgiven; breathe grace!
- Learn from your past. Use the knowledge of events (good and bad) to make wise decisions right now and for future goals. Focus on being more Christlike.
- Don't hang on to parts of your past that pull you down. Once you have repented and confessed, get rid of the reminders—pictures, clothes, movies, music—anything that triggers regret or temptation.

Resources

- "The Faithfulness of God" in *God: As He Longs for You to See Him*. Chip Ingram. Baker.
- *The Hand of God: Finding His Care in All Circumstances* (Life of Joseph). Alistair Begg. Moody.
- "Making All Things New" in *Sex and the Supremacy of Christ*. John Piper and Justin Taylor. Crossway.
- *Moving On: Beyond Forgive and Forget*. Ruth Ann Batstone. New Growth.
- *Putting Your Past Behind You*. Erwin Lutzer. Moody.
- *Putting Your Past in Its Place*. Steve Viars. Harvest House.

Waiting for Sex

See also **Integrity, Self-Control**

You are engaged and looking forward to the intimacies of marriage. But you really do want to wait until after the covenant is made and the ceremony is completed. What are some steps to assist in that wait?

1. **Make a strong commitment as a couple to sexual purity.**

   1 Thessalonians 4:3–5 It is God's will that you should be sanctified: that you should avoid sexual immorality; that each of you should learn to control your own body in a way that is holy and honorable, not in passionate lust like the pagans, who do not know God. (NIV)

   Psalm 119:9–11 How can a young person stay on the path of purity? By living according to your word. I seek you with all my heart; do not let me stray from your commands. I have hidden your word in my heart that I might not sin against you. (NIV)

   Isaiah 50:7 Because the Sovereign Lord helps me, I will not be disgraced. Therefore have I set my face like flint, and I know I will not be put to shame. (NIV)

   Job 31:1

2. **Know that sin comes from inside of ourselves. Be wise to avoid giving in to temptation. Plan your dating and activities to protect and support purity.**

   James 1:13–15 Let no one say when he is tempted, "I am being tempted by God"; for God cannot be tempted by evil, and He Himself does not tempt anyone. But each one is tempted when he is carried away and enticed by his own lust. Then when lust has conceived, it gives birth to sin; and when sin is accomplished, it brings forth death. (NASB)

James 1:5 But if any of you lacks wisdom, let him ask of God, who gives to all generously and without reproach, and it will be given to him. (NASB)

3. **Know that God has provided the means by which we can say no to temptation.**

   1 Corinthians 10:13 No temptation has overtaken you except what is common to mankind. And God is faithful; he will not let you be tempted beyond what you can bear. But when you are tempted, he will also provide a way out so that you can endure it. (NIV)

   Galatians 5:16–17, 24 So I say, walk by the Spirit, and you will not gratify the desires of the flesh. For the flesh desires what is contrary to the Spirit, and the Spirit what is contrary to the flesh. They are in conflict with each other, so that you are not to do whatever you want. . . . Those who belong to Christ Jesus have crucified the flesh with its passions and desires. (NIV)

   Ephesians 6:10–11 Finally, be strong in the Lord and in his mighty power. Put on the full armor of God, so that you can take your stand against the devil's schemes. (NIV)

4. **Focus on the goal of waiting for sex until you are husband and wife. How are you going to implement that plan?**

   1 Corinthians 7:1–3 Now concerning the things about which you wrote, it is good for a man not to touch a woman. But because of immoralities, each man is to have his own wife, and each woman is to have her own husband. The husband must fulfill his duty to his wife, and likewise also the wife to her husband. (NASB)

   Hebrews 12:1–2; 13:4

5. **Spend time with others who will affirm and encourage your commitment to purity. Avoid being alone for longer lengths of time where there might be temptation.**

   2 Timothy 2:22 Flee the evil desires of youth and pursue righteousness, faith, love and peace, along with those who call on the Lord out of a pure heart. (NIV)

Galatians 6:1–2 Brothers and sisters, if someone is caught in a sin, you who live by the Spirit should restore that person gently. But watch yourselves, or you also may be tempted. Carry each other's burdens, and in this way you will fulfill the law of Christ. (NIV)

Proverbs 27:17

6. **Remember that love never takes advantage of another person.**

1 Corinthians 13:4–7 Love is patient, love is kind. It does not envy, it does not boast, it is not proud. It does not dishonor others, it is not self-seeking, it is not easily angered, it keeps no record of wrongs. Love does not delight in evil but rejoices with the truth. It always protects, always trusts, always hopes, always perseveres. (NIV)

1 Thessalonians 4:6–7 And that in this matter no one should wrong or take advantage of a brother or sister. The Lord will punish all those who commit such sins, as we told you and warned you before. For God did not call us to be impure, but to live a holy life. (NIV)

Philippians 2:3–5

Practical Steps

- Set up accountability with Christian friends or mentors.
- Discuss together how you will set your standards, lines you will not cross, what you can do physically, and what you will not do. Know biblical standards and stick with them.
- If you struggle, monitor your time alone. Plan activities in groups.
- Constantly remind yourselves of the goal of beginning marriage with the knowledge that you have waited. Think of the joy you will have that first time together!

Resources

- "Purity Covenant" in *Preparing for Marriage*. Dennis Rainey, ed. Bethany House.

- *Quest for Love*. Elisabeth Elliott. Revell.
- *Sex According to God*. Kay Arthur. WaterBrook.
- *Sex and the Supremacy of Christ*. John Piper and Justin Taylor. Crossway.
- *Sex, Romance, and the Glory of God*. C. J. Mahaney. Crossway.
- "Sexuality" in *Culture Shock*. Chip Ingram. Baker.

Cohabitation

See also **Marriage in the Beginning, Waiting for Sex**

Living together before marriage in a sexually active relationship without legal or religious authority is not a part of God's plan. The idea that cohabitation is not a sin is one of the great lies of today's culture; it is totally unbiblical and part of Satan's plan to destroy the family.

1. **Living together before marriage ignores God's plan for a covenant commitment, (i.e., marriage) first. Consider the use of the word "covenant" in these passages, each referring in some way to marriage.**

   Malachi 2:14–15 Because the Lord was witness between you and the wife of your youth, to whom you have been faithless, though she is your companion and your wife by covenant. Did he not make them one, with a portion of the Spirit in their union? And what was the one God seeking? Godly offspring. So guard yourselves in your spirit, and let none of you be faithless to the wife of your youth. (ESV)

   Proverbs 2:17 [A sinful woman] who has left the partner of her youth and ignored the covenant she made before God. (NIV)

   Ezekiel 16:8 When I passed by you again and saw you, behold, you were at the age for love, and I spread the corner of my garment over you and covered your nakedness; I made my vow to you and entered into a covenant with you, declares the Lord God, and you became mine. (ESV) (God is speaking metaphorically about his choice to make Israel his chosen nation. Israel is viewed as a young woman with whom God made a covenant of marriage.)

2. **Living together and having sex before marriage denies God's order. Scripture is quite clear—covenant, then consummation!**

 Genesis 2:21–25 So the Lord God caused a deep sleep to fall upon the man, and while he slept took one of his ribs and closed up its place with flesh. And the rib that the Lord God had taken from the man he made into a woman and brought her to the man. Then the man said, "This at last is bone of my bones and flesh of my flesh; she shall be called Woman, because she was taken out of Man." Therefore a man shall leave his father and his mother and hold fast to his wife, and they shall become one flesh. And the man and his wife were both naked and were not ashamed. (ESV)

 Proverbs 5:18–19 Let your fountain be blessed, and rejoice in the wife of your youth, a lovely deer, a graceful doe. Let her breasts fill you at all times with delight; be intoxicated always in her love. (ESV)

 Ruth 4:13 So Boaz took Ruth, and she became his wife. And he went in to her, and the Lord gave her conception, and she bore a son. (ESV)

3. **Sexual sin, including intimacy before marriage, is condemned in Scripture and will not lead to God's blessing.**

 1 Corinthians 7:2 But because of the temptation to sexual immorality, each man should have his own wife and each woman her own husband. (ESV)

 1 Thessalonians 4:3–6 For this is the will of God, your sanctification: that you abstain from sexual immorality; that each one of you know how to control his own body in holiness and honor, not in the passion of lust like the Gentiles who do not know God; that no one transgress and wrong his brother in this matter, because the Lord is an avenger in all these things, as we told you beforehand and solemnly warned you. (ESV)

 Hebrews 13:4 Let marriage be held in honor among all, and let the marriage bed be undefiled, for God will judge the sexually immoral and adulterous. (ESV)

 1 Corinthians 6:9

Practical Steps

- Study and consider carefully this definition of covenant—"A covenant is a solemn, sacred agreement, in which persons bind themselves to certain obligations, swearing an oath and signifying in a ceremony the total commitment to fulfill the obligations. The promise is made under God's watchful eye."[1]
- See also the definition of marriage on p. 111 of *Living Together* by Jeff VanGoethem, which helps reinforce the sinful nature of cohabitation.
- Research statistics on relationships ending for those who have cohabited. You will find them to be high.
- Make a commitment to treat the relationship with honor. If you love this person, then value them, honor God's commands, and marry them!
- Remember that repentance and confession of this sin is required. See 1 John 1:6–9.

Resources

- "Marriage as a Covenant in the Bible" in *Living Together: A Guide to Counseling Unmarried Couples*. Jeff VanGoethem. Kregel.
- *True Sexual Morality: Recovering Biblical Standards for a Culture in Crisis*. Daniel Heimbach. Crossway.

1. Jeff VanGoethem, *Living Together: A Guide to Counseling Unmarried Couples* (Grand Rapids: Kregel, 2004), 99.

Part Two

Living in Marriage

So here you are. Two sinners committed to each other for the remainder of your lives. Redeemed sinners, hopefully, but still two imperfect people together in what is the closest of relationships. The honeymoon will eventually be over, and reality will settle in. The key to making this work is the Word of God at work in each of your lives. The remainder of this book takes the essential categories and topics that are applicable to a successful life together and applies the teachings of Scripture for each.

Spiritual Disciplines

A discipline is an "orderly or prescribed conduct or pattern of behavior" (*Merriam-Webster's Collegiate Dictionary*, 11th edition). For the follower of Christ, the spiritual disciplines involve each person spending necessary and consistent time with God, serving him and others. When each spouse follows through with these disciplines, a loving marriage relationship is greatly enhanced. Think of a triangle with God at the top and each person on the bottom right and left. As both get closer to God, each gets closer to the other.

Walking with Christ

See also **Confession, Integrity, Self-Control**

Foundational to our spiritual success is keeping close to Christ. A consistent biblical theme, "walking" (as equivalent to "lifestyle") is how we conduct ourselves as we go through life. Maintaining that relationship with Christ is essential. Here are some basics:

1. **God's words to us through the prophets are insightful for what is needed.**

   Micah 6:8 He has told you, O man, what is good; and what does the Lord require of you but to do justice, and to love kindness, and to walk humbly with your God? (ESV)

2. **A major aspect of this walk experience is remaining close to Christ.**

   John 15:7 If you abide in me, and my words abide in you, ask whatever you wish, and it will be done for you. (ESV)

   John 15:10 If you keep my commandments, you will abide in my love, just as I have kept my Father's commandments and abide in his love. (ESV)

   Deuteronomy 10:12–21; Psalm 91:1–2; John 15:1–11

3. **Jesus is our great example for the walk.**

   1 John 2:6 Whoever says he abides in him ought to walk in the same way in which he walked. (ESV)

   1 Peter 2:21 For to this you have been called, because Christ also suffered for you, leaving you an example, so that you might follow in his steps. (ESV)

   Note his actions—**Philippians 2:5; John 6:38; Mark 10:45**

4. **Depending on the Holy Spirit produces fruit of the Spirit rather than deeds of the flesh.**

   Galatians 5:16 But I say, walk by [means of] the Spirit, and you will not gratify the desires of the flesh. (ESV) (See 5:16–24.)

5. **Learn these specifics for your walk.**

   Romans 6:4 Therefore we have been buried with Him through baptism into death, so that as Christ was raised from the dead through the glory of the Father, so we too might walk in newness of life. (NASB)

   2 Corinthians 5:7 For we walk by faith, not by sight. (NASB)

   Ephesians 5:2 And walk in love, just as Christ also loved you and gave Himself up for us, an offering and a sacrifice to God as a fragrant aroma. (NASB)

   Ephesians 5:8–10 Walk as children of Light (for the fruit of the Light consists in all goodness and righteousness and truth), trying to learn what is pleasing to the Lord. (NASB)

   Genesis 17:1; Joshua 14:7–10; 24:14–15

Practical Steps

- Take time to review what you truly value (relationship with God, spouse, family, health, etc.). Write out goals to help support your values.
- Practice journaling. Writing the events of the day, good and bad, will help remind us of our constant need to walk closely with Christ. Review your thoughts from time to time to check your progress. Evaluate! Examine!
- Daily time spent in the Word and prayer is the key spiritual discipline for maintaining this close walk.
- Charles Ryrie writes that "walking is by its very nature a succession of dependent acts."[2] First, we need to make up our minds to do it. And then "progress can only be made by trusting."

2. Charles Ryrie, *A Survey of Bible Doctrine* (Chicago: Moody Publishers, 1972), 84.

Resources

- *Balancing the Christian Life*. Charles Ryrie. Moody.
- *He That Is Spiritual*. Lewis Sperry Chafer. First Rate Publishers.
- *Pathway to Freedom: How God's Laws Guide Our Lives*. Alistair Begg. Moody.
- *Spiritual Disciplines for the Christian Life*. Donald Whitney. NavPress.
- *True Spirituality: Becoming a Romans 12 Christian*. Chip Ingram. Howard Books.

Essential Disciplines

See also **Decision Making, Priorities**

Maintaining a close relationship with our heavenly Father in obedience to his standards in his Word is vital to spiritual success individually and certainly for a couple aspiring to make their marriage succeed. There are many scriptural and practical ways to ensure continued progress toward that godly maturity. "Essential" here refers to the most basic of those disciplines, the consistent habits of life that will assist in achieving that success.

Discipline for Time Alone with God

1. **Meeting with God alone on a consistent time frame is important (every day, if possible).**

   Psalm 42:1–2 As the deer pants for streams of water, so my soul pants for you, my God. My soul thirsts for God, for the living God. When can I go and meet with God? (NIV)

   Jeremiah 29:13 You will seek me and find me when you seek me with all your heart. (NIV)

   Psalm 63:1; Habakkuk 2:20

2. **Listening to God and waiting on Him gives strength.**

   Psalm 27:14 Wait for the Lord; be strong, and let your heart take courage; wait for the Lord! (ESV)

   Isaiah 40:31 They who wait for the Lord shall renew their strength; they shall mount up with wings like eagles; they shall run and not be weary; they shall walk and not faint. (ESV)

   Psalm 40:1

Discipline for Time in God's Word

1. **Spending time in Scripture—reading, meditation, study—gives direction for each day.**

    Joshua 1:8 This Book of the Law shall not depart from your mouth, but you shall meditate on it day and night, so that you may be careful to do according to all that is written in it. For then you will make your way prosperous, and then you will have good success. (ESV)

    Psalm 119:105 Your word is a lamp to my feet and a light to my path. (ESV)

    Psalm 1:2–3; 19:9–11; 119:129–30; Isaiah 55:1–2; 2 Timothy 3:16–17; Hebrews 4:12

Discipline for Prayer

1. **Spend time communicating/talking to God every day.**

    Psalm 5:2–3 Heed the sound of my cry for help, my King and my God, for to You I pray. In the morning, O Lord, You will hear my voice; in the morning I will order my prayer to You and eagerly watch. (NASB)

    Psalm 88:13; Jeremiah 33:3; Ephesians 6:18; Hebrews 4:16

2. **Prayer is the Christian's lifeline. We must pray—consistently and constantly.**

    Psalm 55:17 Evening, morning and noon I cry out in distress, and he hears my voice. (NIV)

    1 Thessalonians 5:17–18 Pray continually, give thanks in all circumstances; for this is God's will for you in Christ Jesus. (NIV)

    Psalm 86:3–7; Matthew 7:7; Luke 18:1

3. **We can pray about anything that concerns us.**

    Matthew 7:7–11; Philippians 4:6–7

Discipline for Time to Be with Other Believers

1. **Being a part of a local church and attending with consistency is commanded.**

   Hebrews 10:24–25 Let us think of ways to motivate one another to acts of love and good works. And let us not neglect our meeting together, as some people do, but encourage one another, especially now that the day of his return is drawing near. (NLT)
   Psalm 42:4; 122:1; 1 Thessalonians 5:11

2. **In the book of Acts and throughout the letters of the New Testament, the activities of the local church and every believer's involvement is assumed. The church is Christ's bride, and he wants us involved.**

   Acts 13:1; 14:23; Romans 6:5; 1 Corinthians 11:18; 1 Thessalonians 1:1; James 5:14

Discipline for Giving Back to God

1. **Financially supporting your church and Christian ministries is a principle strongly stated in Scripture.**

   2 Corinthians 9:6–8 Whoever sows sparingly will also reap sparingly, and whoever sows generously will also reap generously. Each of you should give what you have decided in your heart to give, not reluctantly or under compulsion, for God loves a cheerful giver. And God is able to bless you abundantly, so that in all things at all times, having all that you need, you will abound in every good work. (NIV)
   Proverbs 3:9 Honor the Lord with your wealth, with the firstfruits of all your crops. (NIV)

2. **While Old Testament tithing is not the law for God's people under the new covenant, the laws of tithing do help us understand God's mind and heart on the question of giving. It represents his thinking on the matter.**

   Leviticus 27:30–33; Malachi 3:8; Romans 6:14–15

Discipline for Furthering the Gospel

1. **Sharing our faith**

   1 Peter 3:15 But have reverence for Christ in your hearts, and honor him as Lord. Be ready at all times to answer anyone who asks you to explain the hope you have in you. (GNT)
   Matthew 5:16; Acts 1:8

2. **Doing good works/bearing fruit**

   Ephesians 2:10 For we are His workmanship, created in Christ Jesus for good works, which God prepared beforehand so that we would walk in them. (NASB)
   John 15:5; Titus 3:8

3. **Helping others who have needs**

   James 1:27 Pure and genuine religion in the sight of God the Father means caring for orphans and widows in their distress and refusing to let the world corrupt you. (NLT)
   Psalm 82:4; Proverbs 31:20; Matthew 25:35; Acts 4:34–35; 2 Corinthians 9:12

4. **Assisting others with heavy burdens**

   Romans 15:1–2 We who are strong ought to bear with the failings of the weak and not to please ourselves. Each of us should please our neighbors for their good, to build them up. (NIV)
   Galatians 6:2

5. **Teaching**

   2 Timothy 2:2 You have heard me teach things that have been confirmed by many reliable witnesses. Now teach these truths to other trustworthy people who will be able to pass them on to others. (NLT)

6. **Leading**

   1 Timothy 3:1 This is a trustworthy saying: "If someone aspires to be a church leader, he desires an honorable position." (NLT)

Practical Steps

- Use music in your time with God. Play worship music and hymns in your home.
- Ideally for a marriage to grow strong, each person must be intentional in their time with God.
- Husbands should take a lead in the spiritual leadership of their family.
- Praying together is one of the best "glues" to bring you solidly together as one in Christ. A good time is when one of you leaves for work or to go on a trip. Commit to the Lord for his care.
- Set up reminders in your cell phone, etc., for taking time in prayer, meditation, solitude, and God's Word.
- Begin at once, right after the wedding, to make giving back to God a part of your budget/financial planning. Do it now!
- Work at keeping Sundays free for local church ministry and involvement. Take a stand with your employers to honor the Lord's Day. Let your leaders know you want to minister.

Resources

- *Basics for Believers: Foundational Truths to Guide Your Life*. William Thrasher. Moody.
- *Good to Great in God's Eyes: 10 Practices Great Christians Have in Common*. Chip Ingram. Baker.
- *A Journey to Victorious Praying*. William Thrasher. Moody.
- *Scripture by Heart: Devotional Practices for Memorizing God's Word*. Joshua Kang. IVP.
- *Spiritual Disciplines for the Christian Life*. Donald Whitney. NavPress.

Personal Walk Issues

In this section, the topics selected all have to do with attitudes and actions for godly, Christlike living. The principles presented are essential to all relationships. However, the emphasis is on marriage, with obedience to Scripture being the key to any success. Here is the central question—what does the Bible teach about maintaining our fruitful relationships with God, others, and our spouse? We must then commit to follow Christ completely and be dependent always on God's Spirit for enablement. The old adage "The closer we are to God, the closer we will be to our spouse" rings true.

Selfishness

See also **Pride, Walking with Christ**

One way to quickly damage a marriage is to constantly think of yourself first and see everything from your own point of view. These two sinful attitudes feed on each other and must be dealt with to ensure a peaceful life together. In a happy, contented marriage, each seeks the other's good and tries to perceive life from the other's perspective.

1. **A beginning point for removing selfishness is to place God at the center of our lives. Loving him takes priority. Focusing on his plan and desires brings his best into our marriage.**

   Matthew 22:37–38 Jesus answered, "'Love the Lord your God with all your heart, with all your soul, and with all your mind.' This is the greatest and the most important commandment." (GNT)

   Luke 9:23–24 And he said to them all, "If you want to come with me, you must forget yourself, take up your cross every day, and follow me. For if you want to save your own life, you will lose it, but if you lose your life for my sake, you will save it." (GNT)

   Matthew 6:33

2. **A self-seeking attitude is sinful and destructive. You don't always have to be right or have the last word.**

   James 3:14–16 But if you harbor bitter envy and selfish ambition in your hearts, do not boast about it or deny the truth. Such "wisdom" does not come down from heaven but is earthly, unspiritual, demonic. For where you have envy and selfish ambition, there you find disorder and every evil practice. (NIV)

Romans 2:8 For those who are self-seeking and do not obey the truth, but obey unrighteousness, there will be wrath and fury. (ESV)

3. **Seeking the best for others is love in action and builds relationships.**

1 Corinthians 13:4–7 Love is patient and kind; it is not jealous or conceited or proud; love is not ill-mannered or selfish or irritable; love does not keep a record of wrongs; love is not happy with evil, but is happy with the truth. Love never gives up; and its faith, hope, and patience never fail. (GNT)

Philippians 2:2–4 I urge you, then, to make me completely happy by having the same thoughts, sharing the same love, and being one in soul and mind. Don't do anything from selfish ambition or from a cheap desire to boast, but be humble toward one another, always considering others better than yourselves. And look out for one another's interests, not just for your own. (GNT)

1 Corinthians 10:24 None of you should be looking out for your own interests, but for the interests of others. (GNT)

Romans 12:10–16

Practical Steps

- Our current culture is so into "It's all about me and my rights" that it becomes difficult to think biblically—"It's all about God and others."
- Evaluate your speech and writing (texts, emails, etc.). How frequently do you use "I, me, my, we, us,"?
- Study/meditate on Romans 12:2, and don't let the world pressure you into its mold.
- Work on thinking of your spouse first and making his or her needs a priority. If you both do this, how beneficial it will be to your marriage!

Resources

- *The Freedom of Self-Forgetfulness*. Timothy Keller. 10Publishing.
- *Self-Centered Spouse: Help for Chronically Broken Marriages*. Brad Hambrick. P&R.
- *Selfishness* (booklet). Lou Priolo. P&R.
- "Selfishness" in *Respectable Sins*. Jerry Bridges. NavPress.
- *When Sinners Say "I Do."* Dave Harvey. Shepherd.

Self-Control

See also **Contentment, Materialism, Finances, Purity, Temptation**

Self-control includes the qualities of restraint, non-impulsive behavior, thinking through one's options before acting, and delayed gratification. Discipline, a corollary, includes careful planning, staying the course, and doing what is needed to accomplish the task. A lack of these qualities in marriage is a blueprint for disaster.

1. **Lack of self-control leads to broken lives and marriages. Such sinful attitudes and behaviors are destructive.**

   Proverbs 25:28 A person without self-control is like a city with broken-down walls. (NLT)

   2 Timothy 3:1–4 But understand this, that in the last days there will come times of difficulty. For people will be lovers of self, lovers of money, proud, arrogant, abusive, disobedient to their parents, ungrateful, unholy, heartless, unappeasable, slanderous, without self-control, brutal, not loving good, treacherous, reckless, swollen with conceit, lovers of pleasure rather than lovers of God. (ESV)

   1 Peter 1:13–16

2. **Control your tongue! What we say is important, but also how we say it—tone and body language.**

   James 3:5 So also the tongue is a small member, yet it boasts of great things. How great a forest is set ablaze by such a small fire! (ESV)

   Proverbs 12:18 There is one whose rash words are like sword thrusts, but the tongue of the wise brings healing. (ESV)

Proverbs 17:27 A truly wise person uses few words; a person with understanding is even-tempered. (NLT)

Proverbs 10:19; 12:19; 29:11; 29:20

3. **Knowing and obeying God's Word is vital to maintaining self-control.**

   Joshua 1:8 This Book of the Law shall not depart from your mouth, but you shall meditate on it day and night, so that you may be careful to do according to all that is written in it. For then you will make your way prosperous, and then you will have good success. (ESV)

   Psalm 119:101–3 I have restrained my feet from every evil way, that I may keep Your word. I have not turned aside from Your ordinances, for You Yourself have taught me. How sweet are Your words to my taste! Yes, sweeter than honey to my mouth! (NASB)

   Psalm 119:9–11 How can a young man keep his way pure? By keeping it according to Your word. With all my heart I have sought You; do not let me wander from Your commandments. Your word I have treasured in my heart, that I may not sin against You. (NASB)

   Proverbs 6:23; 2 Timothy 3:16–17

4. **We must depend on God's Spirit, accepting his control in our lives.**

   Galatians 5:16 But I say, walk by [by means of, depend on] the Spirit, and you will not gratify the desires of the flesh. (ESV)

   Ephesians 5:18 Don't be drunk with wine, because that will ruin your life. Instead, be filled with the Holy Spirit. (NLT) (The issue is what controls us: the things of this world or God?)

Practical Steps

- If you aim at nothing, you will be sure to hit it. Make specific plans, with set goals and objectives. Establish a time each week to evaluate improvement.

- Whatever the area in which there is a lack of self-control, seek accountability with your spouse. Communicate with each other often to confess, pray, and discuss progress.
- Always take time together to list "pros and cons" before making any decision.
- If you have a history together of making decisions too quickly, set a specific time frame for thinking and discussing the issue before a final determination is made.
- If financial decisions are an area of concern, study together Paul's take on money from 1 Timothy 6:6–19 and/or Jesus's words from Matthew 6:19–24.

Resources

- *Disciplines of a Godly Man*. Kent Hughes. Crossway.
- "Lack of Self-Control" in *Respectable Sins*. Jerry Bridges. NavPress.
- *Motives: Why Do I Do the Things I Do* (booklet). Ed Welch. P&R.

Pride

See also **Materialism, Priorities, Self-Worth**

Sinful pride is taking credit away from God for who we are, what we have accomplished, how we look, what we own, or our position/status in life. It often involves looking down on others. Like any sin issue, it is a detriment to our personal walk in addition to our functioning well as a couple who desires to live in obedience to God.

1. **God is not pleased with pride, but humility is his delight.**

   Psalm 101:5 Whoever has a haughty look and an arrogant heart I will not endure. (ESV)

   Proverbs 21:4 Haughty eyes and a proud heart, the lamp of the wicked, are sin. (ESV)

   Proverbs 8:13 The fear of the Lord is hatred of evil. Pride and arrogance and the way of evil and perverted speech I hate. (ESV)

   James 4:6 But He gives more grace. Therefore He says: "God resists the proud, but gives grace to the humble." (NKJV)

   Psalm 18:27; 138:6; Proverbs 3:34; 16:19; 26:12

2. **Pride leads to humiliation, conflict, even destruction.**

   Psalm 18:27 You rescue the humble, but you humiliate the proud. (NLT)

   Proverbs 13:10 Pride leads to conflict; those who take advice are wise. (NLT)

   Proverbs 16:18 Pride goes before destruction, and haughtiness before a fall. (NLT)

   Isaiah 2:11 Human pride will be brought down, and human arrogance will be humbled. Only the Lord will be exalted on that day of judgment. (NLT)

   Mark 7:20–23

3. **There is only one boasting that pleases God—praise directed to him.**

 Jeremiah 9:23–24 Thus says the Lord: "Let not the wise man boast in his wisdom, let not the mighty man boast in his might, let not the rich man boast in his riches, but let him who boasts boast in this, that he understands and knows me, that I am the Lord who practices steadfast love, justice, and righteousness in the earth. For in these things I delight, declares the Lord." (ESV)

 Psalm 44:8; Galatians 6:14

4. **We must recognize that all we have and all we do comes directly from God.**

 1 Corinthians 15:10 But by the grace of God I am what I am, and his grace to me was not without effect. No, I worked harder than all of them—yet not I, but the grace of God that was with me. (NIV)

 1 Timothy 6:17 As for the rich in this present age, charge them not to be haughty, nor to set their hopes on the uncertainty of riches, but on God, who richly provides us with everything to enjoy. (ESV)

 Deuteronomy 8:11–14; John 15:5; 1 Corinthians 3:1–9

5. **Pride should be replaced by humility.**

 Philippians 2:3–4 Don't be selfish; don't try to impress others. Be humble, thinking of others as better than yourselves. Don't look out only for your own interests, but take an interest in others, too. (NLT)

 Romans 12:3 For by the grace given to me I say to everyone among you not to think of himself more highly than he ought to think, but to think with sober judgment, each according to the measure of faith that God has assigned. (ESV)

 1 Peter 5:5; 1 John 2:15–17

6. **Humility brings God's approval.**

 Micah 6:8 He has told you, O man, what is good; and what does the Lord require of you but to do justice, and to love kindness, and to walk humbly with your God? (ESV)

Psalm 51:17 The sacrifices of God are a broken spirit; a broken and contrite heart, O God, you will not despise. (ESV)

Practical Steps

- Keep the thought before you—"God owns it all; everything we have comes from him."
- As you pray together always begin with several areas of thanksgiving. Make a list of accomplishments and possessions for which you could be proud. Then, going through each item, speak to each other as to why each of these comes from the hand of God. Make this a time of praise and thanksgiving!
- Memorize Jeremiah 9:23–24. Type it on a card, and keep it handy for a reminder.
- Memorize Philippians 2:3–4. Review these verses often when you are tempted to feel you are always right, or better than others.

Resources

- *From Pride to Humility*. Stuart Scott. Focus.
- *Humility: The Forgotten Virtue* (booklet). Wayne Mack. P&R.
- *Humility: The True Greatness*. C. J. Mahaney. Multnomah.
- "Pride" in *Respectable Sins*. Jerry Bridges. NavPress.

Thought Life

See also **Anxiety, Fantasizing, Materialism, Temptation**

Making sure our thoughts are pleasing to God is one of the great challenges for the Christian life. No human being knows what we are thinking but, of course, God does. Impure, immature, or selfish thinking will bring injury to the marriage relationship. Asking God to bring our thought life under his control is crucial.

1. **While no other human being knows what we are thinking, God always knows.**

   Psalm 139:1–4 O Lord, you have examined my heart and know everything about me. You know when I sit down or stand up. You know my thoughts even when I'm far away. You see me when I travel and when I rest at home. You know everything I do. You know what I am going to say even before I say it, Lord. (NLT)

   Jeremiah 23:23–24 "Am I a God who is only close at hand?" says the Lord. "No, I am far away at the same time. Can anyone hide from me in a secret place? Am I not everywhere in all the heavens and earth?" says the Lord. (NLT)

   Hebrews 4:13 Nothing in all creation is hidden from God. Everything is naked and exposed before his eyes, and he is the one to whom we are accountable. (NLT)

2. **Sacrificial thinking will place our spouse's needs before our needs and is a must for the marriage relationship.**

   1 Corinthians 13:4–7 Love is patient and kind. Love is not jealous or boastful or proud or rude. It does not demand its own way. It is not irritable, and it keeps no record of being wronged. It does not rejoice about injustice but rejoices whenever the truth wins out. Love never gives up, never loses faith, is always hopeful, and endures through every circumstance. (NLT)

1 Corinthians 10:24 Don't be concerned for your own good but for the good of others. (NLT)

Philippians 2:4–7 Don't look out only for your own interests, but take an interest in others, too. You must have the same attitude that Christ Jesus had. Though he was God, he did not think of equality with God as something to cling to. Instead, he gave up his divine privileges; he took the humble position of a slave and was born as a human being. (NLT)

Philippians 2:21

3. **Mature/wise thinking is necessary for your marriage relationship.**

1 Corinthians 13:11 When I was a child, my speech, feelings, and thinking were all those of a child; now that I am an adult, I have no more use for childish ways. (GNT)

1 Corinthians 14:20 Do not be like children in your thinking, my friends; be children so far as evil is concerned, but be grown up in your thinking. (GNT)

4. **Prideful thoughts are not pleasing to God and are a hindrance to any relationship.**

Psalm 138:6 Though the Lord is great, he cares for the humble, but he keeps his distance from the proud. (NLT)

James 4:6 But he gives more grace. Therefore it says, "God opposes the proud, but gives grace to the humble." (ESV)

Proverbs 13:10 Pride leads to conflict; those who take advice are wise. (NLT)

Proverbs 16:18 Pride goes before destruction, and haughtiness before a fall. (NLT)

5. **Our thoughts must be placed under God's control.**

Psalm 19:14 Let the words of my mouth and the meditation of my heart be acceptable in your sight, O Lord, my rock and my redeemer. (ESV)

2 Corinthians 10:4–5 For the weapons of our warfare are not of the flesh, but divinely powerful for the destruction of fortresses. We are destroying speculations and every lofty thing raised up against the knowledge of God, and we are taking every thought captive to the obedience of Christ. (NASB)

Ephesians 5:18; Hebrews 4:12

6. **We are responsible for monitoring our thinking, emphasizing the positive rather than the negative.**

   Philippians 4:8 And now, dear brothers and sisters, one final thing. Fix your thoughts on what is true, and honorable, and right, and pure, and lovely, and admirable. Think about things that are excellent and worthy of praise. (NLT)

Practical Steps

- List four areas where your thoughts toward your spouse have not been sacrificial. Then consider specific actions you can take to correct these to become more loving in your attitudes and actions.
- Do not assume that your thoughts or attitudes are as they should be. Evaluate and ask your spouse what would be helpful.
- Compare your thinking to the specific scriptural commands/principles listed above. How are you matching up to God's standards? Make sure you are not justifying inappropriate attitudes with a misapplication of his Word.
- Keep each other accountable to be positive in your thinking (Philippians 4:8). Continual negative thinking will be destructive to your relationship.

Resources

- *Changing Your Thought Patterns* (booklet). George Sanchez. NavPress.
- *How People Change*. Timothy Lane. New Growth.

- *Lies Women Believe*. Nancy Leigh DeMoss. Moody.
- *Right Thinking in a World Gone Wrong*. John MacArthur. Harvest House.
- *You Can Change: God's Transforming Power for Our Sinful Behavior and Negative Emotions*. Tim Chester. Crossway.

Integrity

See also **Self-Control, Temptation**

For the Christian, integrity is firm adherence to God's righteous standards—standing for the right because it is the right thing to do—no matter what, no matter when. Honesty and openness are marks of integrity; related qualities include sincerity, accountability, justice, faithfulness, and responsibility. These character qualities are a notable goal for every married couple.

1. **God is looking for people of character and integrity who will make a difference in our world for his kingdom. Will your marriage make that difference?**

   2 Chronicles 16:9 For the eyes of the Lord move to and fro throughout the earth that He may strongly support those whose heart is completely His. (NASB)

   Isaiah 42:6 I, the Lord, have called you to demonstrate my righteousness. I will take you by the hand and guard you. (NLT)

   Ezekiel 22:30

2. **A man and woman whose marriage gives strong evidence of moral, ethical, and spiritual character can expect God's best for their marriage.**

   Psalm 25:21 May integrity and uprightness protect me, because my hope, Lord, is in you. (NIV)

   Proverbs 13:6 Righteousness guards the person of integrity, but wickedness overthrows the sinner. (NIV)

   Proverbs 10:9 Whoever walks in integrity walks securely, but whoever takes crooked paths will be found out. (NIV)

   Proverbs 2:7–11 He grants a treasure of common sense to the honest. He is a shield to those who walk with integrity. He guards the paths of the just and protects those who are faithful to him. Then you will understand what is right, just, and fair, and you will find the right way to go. For wisdom will enter your heart, and knowledge will fill you with joy. Wise choices will watch over you. Understanding will keep you safe. (NLT)

Psalm 37:3

3. **The integrity of obedience to God's Word will bring joy to our lives.**

   Psalm 119:1–3 Joyful are people of integrity, who follow the instructions of the Lord. Joyful are those who obey his laws and search for him with all their hearts. They do not compromise with evil, and they walk only in his paths. (NLT)

4. **God is pleased when we are men and women of integrity. He blesses us when we obey.**

   1 Chronicles 29:17 I know, my God, that you test the heart and are pleased with integrity. (NIV)

   Psalm 15:1–2 Who may worship in your sanctuary, Lord? Who may enter your presence on your holy hill? Those who lead blameless lives and do what is right, speaking the truth from sincere hearts. (NLT)

   Proverbs 11:3 The integrity of the upright guides them, but the crookedness of the treacherous destroys them. (ESV)

   Matthew 5:6–9 Blessed are those who hunger and thirst for righteousness, for they shall be filled. Blessed are the merciful, for they shall obtain mercy. Blessed are the pure in heart, for they shall see God. Blessed are the peacemakers, for they shall be called sons of God. (NKJV)

   Isaiah 33:15–16

Practical Steps

- Use Bible study tools to do a word study of "integrity." The NASB has twenty-seven occurrences of the word. Note lack of integrity in some instances, as well as positive examples.

- When making decisions that will reflect on your integrity, pray for strength and wisdom, while making a solid pledge to stand for the right. Seek accountability from others.
- Integrity is holding to truth and commitment even when we are alone, out of town, when no one is watching. Ask yourself if you are consistently obedient to God.

Resources

- *Character That Counts: Who's Counting Yours?* Rod Handley. Cross Training.
- "Discipline of Integrity" in *Disciplines of a Godly Man.* Kent Hughes. Crossway.
- "Discipline of Marriage" in *Disciplines of a Godly Woman.* Barbara Hughes. Crossway.
- *Lasting Love: How to Avoid Marital Failure.* Alistair Begg. Moody.
- *The Quest for Character.* John MacArthur. Thomas Nelson.

Contentment

See also **Finances, Loving Him—Loving Her, Materialism, Temptation**

In a marriage context, contentment would include resolving to be satisfied with the marriage partner you have chosen and not nagging or attempting to change the other. Also included would be the resolve to not pressure one's spouse if material possessions are less than we would like. The Old Testament use of the word "blessed" includes happiness, rest, thankfulness, and relaxation of spirit. Contentment in the New Testament means "having enough or a sufficient supply."

1. **Couples might be tempted to compare what they have with others who seem to be more prosperous. Note this example from Psalm writer Asaph.**

   Psalm 73:2–3, 16–17, 25–26 But I had nearly lost confidence; my faith was almost gone because I was jealous of the proud when I saw that things go well for the wicked. . . . I tried to think this problem through, but it was too difficult for me until I went into your Temple. Then I understood what will happen to the wicked. . . . What else do I have in heaven but you? Since I have you, what else could I want on earth? My mind and my body may grow weak, but God is my strength; he is all I ever need. (GNT)

   Psalm 37:7, 16 Be patient and wait for the Lord to act; don't be worried about those who prosper or those who succeed in their evil plans. . . . The little that a good person owns is worth more than the wealth of all the wicked. (GNT)

   Proverbs 15:16–17

2. **Contentment is delighting in our heavenly Father no matter our circumstances.**

   Psalm 36:7–9 How precious is your unfailing love, O God! All humanity finds shelter in the shadow of your wings. You feed them from the abundance of your own house, letting them drink from your river of delights. For you are the fountain of life, the light by which we see. (NLT)

   Psalm 94:19 When my anxious thoughts multiply within me, Your consolations delight my soul. (NASB)

   Psalm 111:2–5 How amazing are the deeds of the Lord! All who delight in him should ponder them. Everything he does reveals his glory and majesty. His righteousness never fails. He causes us to remember his wonderful works. How gracious and merciful is our Lord! He gives food to those who fear him; he always remembers his covenant. (NLT)

   Psalm 84:10–12 A single day in your courts is better than a thousand anywhere else! I would rather be a gatekeeper in the house of my God than live the good life in the homes of the wicked. For the Lord God is our sun and our shield. He gives us grace and glory. The Lord will withhold no good thing from those who do what is right. O Lord of Heaven's Armies, what joy for those who trust in you. (NLT)

   Psalm 118:24; 2 Corinthians 12:9–10

3. **Contentment is resting with confidence in the Lord's provision. This trust removes the tension of discontent.**

   Ecclesiastes 2:24–25 A person can do nothing better than to eat and drink and find satisfaction in their own toil. This too, I see, is from the hand of God, for without him, who can eat or find enjoyment? (NIV)

   1 Timothy 6:6–8 Yet true godliness with contentment is itself great wealth. After all, we brought nothing with us when we came into the world, and we can't take anything with us when we leave it. So if we have enough food and clothing, let us be content. (NLT)

   Isaiah 26:3–4; Philippians 4:19

4. **Contentment and thankfulness, whether with material possessions or personal needs, should be every couple's goal.**

Psalm 107:8–9 Let them thank the LORD for his steadfast love, for his wondrous works to the children of man! For he satisfies the longing soul, and the hungry soul he fills with good things. (ESV)

Hebrews 13:5 Keep your lives free from the love of money, and be satisfied with what you have. For God has said, "I will never leave you; I will never abandon you." (GNT)

Proverbs 16:8 Better is a little with righteousness than great revenues with injustice. (ESV)

Philippians 4:11–13 And I am not saying this because I feel neglected, for I have learned to be satisfied with what I have. I know what it is to be in need and what it is to have more than enough. I have learned this secret, so that anywhere, at any time, I am content, whether I am full or hungry, whether I have too much or too little. I have the strength to face all conditions by the power that Christ gives me. (GNT)

Proverbs 17:1

5. **Being content with who we are in Christ will help us be content with our present life status. An improved sense of self-worth is also a result.**

Jeremiah 9:23–24 Thus says the LORD: "Let not the wise man glory in his wisdom, let not the mighty man glory in his might, nor let the rich man glory in his riches; but let him who glories glory in this, that he understands and knows Me, that I am the LORD, exercising lovingkindness, judgment, and righteousness in the earth. For in these I delight," says the LORD. (NKJV)

Ephesians 1:3–4 Praise be to the God and Father of our Lord Jesus Christ, who has blessed us in the heavenly realms with every spiritual blessing in Christ. For he chose us in him before the creation of the world to be holy and blameless in his sight. (NIV)

Ephesians 2:4–7 But because of his great love for us, God, who is rich in mercy, made us alive with Christ even when we were dead in transgressions—it is by grace you have been saved.

> And God raised us up with Christ and seated us with him in the heavenly realms in Christ Jesus, in order that in the coming ages he might show the incomparable riches of his grace, expressed in his kindness to us in Christ Jesus. (NIV)

Practical Steps

- Avoid window shopping, whether in stores or online, or looking at the new cars when having your car worked on. Why tempt yourself?
- Clear your attic, garage, and closets of items you no longer use—give to a charitable cause. This will help you realize that life doesn't consist of "stuff."
- Study the word "blessing" in the Psalms. The meaning of the word essentially equals "contentment." Look for the phrase "Blessed is the one who . . ." Study and discover!
- Keep a "thankful list"—write down the big and small blessings. Keep this in your Bible, and when discontentment settles in, review your list.
- Before you buy something, ask—will this really be beneficial to my family? Do we really need this? Avoid the urge for the newer, bigger, and better. Update only when an item wears out.
- Be thankful for the skills, talents, and abilities you have received as blessings from God. Don't fall into the trap of "if God had just given me this . . . or blessed me there . . . then life would have been good."

Resources

- *Choosing Gratitude*. Nancy Leigh DeMoss. Moody.
- *Discontentment: Why Am I So Unhappy?* Lou Priolo. P&R.
- "Discontentment" in *Respectable Sins*. Jerry Bridges. NavPress.
- "Learning Generosity" in *The Measure of a Man*. Gene Getz. Revell.
- *The Secret of Contentment*. William J. Barclay. P&R.
- "Your Struggle with Contentment" in *The 10 Greatest Struggles of Your Life*. Colin S. Smith. Moody.

Entertainment

See also **Decision Making, Finances, Priorities, Temptation**

There is so much to enjoy in our world for our leisure time. Some of the issues involved are the need to make godly choices, the amount of time that should be spent, and weighing the financial cost. Consider entertainment that can be enjoyed as a couple/family as opposed to that which pulls you away from your family.

1. **Couples must consistently pursue what is right, making entertainment decisions that are pleasing to God.**

   Psalm 101:2–4 I will be careful to live a blameless life—when will you come to help me? I will lead a life of integrity in my own home. I will refuse to look at anything vile and vulgar. I hate all who deal crookedly; I will have nothing to do with them. I will reject perverse ideas and stay away from every evil. (NLT)

   2 Timothy 2:22 Run from anything that stimulates youthful lusts. Instead, pursue righteous living, faithfulness, love, and peace. Enjoy the companionship of those who call on the Lord with pure hearts. (NLT)

   Colossians 3:5–6 So put to death the sinful, earthly things lurking within you. Have nothing to do with sexual immorality, impurity, lust, and evil desires. Don't be greedy, for a greedy person is an idolater, worshiping the things of this world. (NLT)

   Joshua 24:14; Galatians 5:16; Philippians 4:8; 3 John 11

2. **We must remember that although everything God has created is good, Satan has his counterfeit and corrupt system of worldly pleasures, and he would use these to cause problems in our marriage.**

God's Wonderful Creation

Psalm 8:1, 3–4 O Lord, our Lord, how majestic is your name in all the earth! You have set your glory above the heavens. . . . When I look at your heavens, the work of your fingers, the moon and the stars, which you have set in place, what is man that you are mindful of him, and the son of man that you care for him? (ESV)

1 Chronicles 29:11 Yours, O Lord, is the greatness and the power and the glory and the victory and the majesty, for all that is in the heavens and in the earth is yours. Yours is the kingdom, O Lord, and you are exalted as head above all. (ESV)

Revelation 4:11 Worthy are you, our Lord and God, to receive glory and honor and power, for you created all things, and by your will they existed and were created. (ESV)

Genesis 1:27–31

Satan's Corrupt Counterfeit

Genesis 3:1–5 Now the serpent was more crafty than any other beast of the field that the Lord God had made. He said to the woman, "Did God actually say, 'You shall not eat of any tree in the garden'?" And the woman said to the serpent, "We may eat of the fruit of the trees in the garden, but God said, 'You shall not eat of the fruit of the tree that is in the midst of the garden, neither shall you touch it, lest you die.'" But the serpent said to the woman, "You will not surely die. For God knows that when you eat of it your eyes will be opened, and you will be like God, knowing good and evil." (ESV)

John 8:44 For you are the children of your father the devil, and you love to do the evil things he does. He was a murderer from the beginning. He has always hated the truth, because there is no truth in him. When he lies, it is consistent with his character; for he is a liar and the father of lies. (NLT)

1 John 5:19 We know that we are of God, and that the whole world lies in the power of the evil one. (NASB)

1 John 2:15–17 Do not love the world nor the things in the world. If anyone loves the world, the love of the Father is not in him. For all that is in the world, the lust of the flesh and the lust of the eyes and the boastful pride of life, is not from the Father, but is from the world. The world is passing away, and also its lusts; but the one who does the will of God lives forever. (NASB)

Galatians 5:19–21; Ephesians 5:4; Colossians 2:8; 2 Corinthians 11:14

3. **We must be wise in our use of time. Any entertainment activity can be practiced to an extreme.**

Psalm 90:12 So teach us to number our days, that we may present to You a heart of wisdom. (NASB)

Ephesians 5:15–17 Therefore be careful how you walk, not as unwise men but as wise, making the most of your time, because the days are evil. So then do not be foolish, but understand what the will of the Lord is. (NASB)

Titus 3:8 The saying is trustworthy, and I want you to insist on these things, so that those who have believed in God may be careful to devote themselves to good works. These things are excellent and profitable for people. (ESV)

Practical Steps

- For a better use of time, read quality books out loud with each other.
- Plan mostly couple-oriented activities that both of you can enjoy and be involved in.
- As a couple, discuss the time each of you spends in individual entertainment. Set goals and limits, and be specific. Is one person having to pull a greater load in the marriage because the other is spending too much time reading or gaming? Consider also the question of balancing financial cost.
- If computer sites are a problem, add accountability software or filters.
- Look over your movie and game library, evaluating what is God-honoring. Remove what is not.
- Visit Christian websites to evaluate movies before viewing.

- Keep a record of how much time each day is spent on an activity. This can be eye-opening.
- Consider community offerings for art, museums, concerts, and theater. Choose the positive, godly presentations.
- If you have moved into sinful areas and improper images, work on deleting these from the "hard drive" of your mind through saturation with Scripture. Take needed steps towards accountability and freedom. Repent and confess as needed.

Resources

- *Breaking the Addictive Cycle* (booklet). David Powlison. New Growth.
- *Hope & Help for Video Game, TV, and Internet Addiction* (booklet). Mark Shaw. Focus.
- "Life in the Real World" in *Age of Opportunity*. Paul Tripp. P&R.
- *Living the Cross Centered Life*. C. J. Mahaney. Multnomah.
- *Worldly Amusements: Restoring the Lordship of Christ to Our Entertainment Choices.* Wayne Wilson. WinePress.

Confession

See also **Forgiving Each Other, Forgiveness from God, Handling the Past**

After the dust settles and the wedding and honeymoon are past, reality sets in. Here are two sinners (hopefully both redeemed in Christ—see "Gospel") living together, eating, sleeping, conversing, working, playing together. Until Jesus comes back, the old flesh is ever present and active. Sin happens—a regrettable fact of life. And when it does, it is important to the marriage relationship for repentance and confession to take place—for our personal walk with Christ and for walking together in harmony.

1. **We might be able to hide our sins from our spouse for a time, but hiding sin from God is never possible. He knows exactly what we have done!**

   Numbers 32:23 Be sure your sin will find you out. (ESV)

   Psalm 139:1–4, 7–12 O Lord, you have searched me and known me! You know when I sit down and when I rise up; you discern my thoughts from afar. You search out my path and my lying down and are acquainted with all my ways. Even before a word is on my tongue, behold, O Lord, you know it altogether. . . . Where shall I go from your Spirit? Or where shall I flee from your presence? If I ascend to heaven, you are there! If I make my bed in Sheol, you are there! If I take the wings of the morning and dwell in the uttermost parts of the sea, even there your hand shall lead me, and your right hand shall hold me. If I say, "Surely the darkness shall cover me, and the light about me be night," even the darkness is not dark to you; the night is bright as the day, for darkness is as light with you. (ESV)

   Isaiah 59:12–13 For our transgressions are multiplied before you, and our sins testify against us; for our transgressions are with us, and we know our iniquities: transgressing, and denying the Lord, and turning back from following our God, speaking oppression and revolt, conceiving and uttering from the heart lying words. (ESV)

2. **Freely admitting our sin is the only path to forgiveness and freedom from guilt. Repentance and confession must take place. This will only make the marriage stronger.**

Psalm 32:3–5 When I kept silent about my sin, my body wasted away through my groaning all day long. For day and night Your hand was heavy upon me; my vitality was drained away as with the fever heat of summer. I acknowledged my sin to You, and my iniquity I did not hide; I said, "I will confess my transgressions to the Lord"; and You forgave the guilt of my sin. (NASB)

Psalm 41:4 As for me, I said, "O Lord, be gracious to me; heal my soul, for I have sinned against you." (NASB)

Joel 2:12–13 "But even now," says the Lord, "repent sincerely and return to me with fasting and weeping and mourning. Let your broken heart show your sorrow; tearing your clothes is not enough." Come back to the Lord your God. He is kind and full of mercy; he is patient and keeps his promise; he is always ready to forgive and not punish. (GNT)

Hosea 14:1–2

3. **Confession of sin involves a commitment to stop that sin and be done with it.**

Proverbs 28:13 Whoever conceals his transgressions will not prosper, but he who confesses and forsakes them will obtain mercy. (ESV)

Isaiah 1:16 Wash yourselves; make yourselves clean; remove the evil of your deeds from before my eyes; cease to do evil. (ESV)

Ezekiel 18:30–31 Therefore I will judge you, O house of Israel, every one according to his ways, declares the Lord God. Repent and turn from all your transgressions, lest iniquity be your ruin. Cast away from you all the transgressions that you have committed, and make yourselves a new heart and a new spirit! Why will you die, O house of Israel? (ESV)

4. **Keeping "short accounts" with God and with our spouse (not letting the matter go on and on) is the best path. Restoration and healing are available.**

   1 John 1:9 If we confess our sins, he is faithful and just to forgive us our sins and to cleanse us from all unrighteousness. (ESV)

   Psalm 51:9–12 Hide your face from my sins, and blot out all my iniquities. Create in me a clean heart, O God, and renew a right spirit within me. Cast me not away from your presence, and take not your Holy Spirit from me. Restore to me the joy of your salvation, and uphold me with a willing spirit. (ESV)

   Jeremiah 24:7 I will give them a heart to know Me, for I am the Lord; and they will be My people, and I will be their God, for they will return to Me with their whole heart. (NASB)

   Psalm 66:18; Malachi 3:7

5. **Confession of sin may require restitution or making things right with people we have wronged. We must take steps, even if it is difficult, to restore to those we have wronged. Patience for healing of the wound is needed.**

   1 Corinthians 13:4–5 Love is patient, love is kind and is not jealous; love does not brag and is not arrogant, does not act unbecomingly; it does not seek its own, is not provoked, does not take into account a wrong suffered. (NASB)

   Proverbs 14:9 Fools mock at making amends for sin, but goodwill is found among the upright. (NIV)

   Matthew 5:23–24 So if you are about to offer your gift to God at the altar and there you remember that your brother has something against you, leave your gift there in front of the altar, go at once and make peace with your brother, and then come back and offer your gift to God. (GNT)

   James 5:16 Confess your sins to each other and pray for each other so that you may be healed. The earnest prayer of a righteous person has great power and produces wonderful results. (NLT)

   Leviticus 6:1–5; Numbers 5:6–7; Luke 19:8

Practical Steps

- Make a list of what God does with confessed sin. See Psalm 103:12; Isaiah 1:18; 38:17; 44:22; Hebrews 8:12; Micah 7:18–20.
- Remind yourself that it is for your sin that Jesus died.
- Journal your thankfulness to God.
- When we confess sin, what is God's response to us from the following passages: Psalm 32:1; 51:12; 103:10–13; Isaiah 55:7; Romans 8:1–2; 2 Corinthians 5:17?
- Model your forgiveness of others to reflect how God has forgiven you.

Resources

- "Confessing and Forgiving" in *Balancing the Christian Life*. Charles Ryrie. Moody.
- *The Prodigal God: Recovering the Heart of the Christian Faith*. Timothy Keller. Dutton.
- "The Remedy for Sin" in *Respectable Sins*. Jerry Bridges. NavPress.
- "When You've Blown It Big Time" in *Finding God When You Need Him Most*. Chip Ingram. Baker.

Forgiveness from God

See also **Confession, Forgiving Each Other, Walking with Christ**

Sin is the plague of all mankind; no one is exempt. Those who come to Christ in faith are forgiven, cleansed, and made a part of God's family. Yet as Christians, we still live in these bodies and the old nature causes sin. Resisting temptation is the goal, but we do fail. Sin happens, unfortunately. The good news is that God does forgive.

1. **Notice the joy and relief when our sins are forgiven!**

   Isaiah 12:1–4 You will say in that day: "I will give thanks to you, O Lord, for though you were angry with me, your anger turned away, that you might comfort me. Behold, God is my salvation; I will trust, and will not be afraid; for the Lord God is my strength and my song, and he has become my salvation." With joy you will draw water from the wells of salvation. And you will say in that day: "Give thanks to the Lord, call upon his name, make known his deeds among the peoples, proclaim that his name is exalted." (ESV) (See also 1 John 2:2, and note that *propitiation* means "anger turned away.")

2. **Whatever the sin, God is willing to forgive. This is cause for great gladness and thankfulness!**

   Psalm 130:3–4 If you, O Lord, should mark iniquities, O Lord, who could stand? But with you there is forgiveness, that you may be feared. (ESV)

   Lamentations 3:22 The Lord's lovingkindnesses indeed never cease, for His compassions never fail. (NASB)

   Psalm 86:5 For you, O Lord, are good and forgiving, abounding in steadfast love to all who call upon you. (ESV)

Romans 8:1–2 There is therefore now no condemnation for those who are in Christ Jesus. For the law of the Spirit of life has set you free in Christ Jesus from the law of sin and death. (ESV)

Daniel 9:9

3. **Our part is to repent and confess our sin to God, who will then forgive and cleanse.**

1 John 1:9 If we confess our sins, he is faithful and just to forgive us our sins and to cleanse us from all unrighteousness. (ESV)

Proverbs 28:13 Whoever conceals their sins does not prosper, but the one who confesses and renounces them finds mercy. (NIV)

Psalm 32:5 Then I acknowledged my sin to you and did not cover up my iniquity. I said, "I will confess my transgressions to the Lord." And you forgave the guilt of my sin. (NIV)

Acts 3:19 Repent, then, and turn to God, so that your sins may be wiped out, that times of refreshing may come from the Lord. (NIV)

Psalm 51:1–2 Have mercy on me, O God, according to your unfailing love; according to your great compassion blot out my transgressions. Wash away all my iniquity and cleanse me from my sin. (NIV)

Isaiah 55:6–7 Seek the Lord while he may be found; call upon him while he is near; let the wicked forsake his way, and the unrighteous man his thoughts; let him return to the Lord, that he may have compassion on him, and to our God, for he will abundantly pardon. (ESV)

Psalm 25:7; 38:18; 66:18–19

4. **God not only forgives; he also supplies complete restoration.**

Psalm 103:10–11 He has not dealt with us according to our sins, nor punished us according to our iniquities. For as the heavens are high above the earth, so great is His mercy toward those who fear Him. (NKJV)

Colossians 1:13–14 For he has rescued us from the kingdom of darkness and transferred us into the Kingdom of his dear Son, who purchased our freedom and forgave our sins. (NLT)

Romans 8:1–2 There is therefore now no condemnation for those who are in Christ Jesus. For the law of the Spirit of life has set you free in Christ Jesus from the law of sin and death. (ESV)

2 Corinthians 5:17 Therefore, if anyone is in Christ, he is a new creation. The old has passed away; behold, the new has come. (ESV)

Psalm 51:12 Restore to me the joy of your salvation, and uphold me with a willing spirit. (ESV)

Psalm 130:7 Israel, put your hope in the LORD, for with the LORD is unfailing love and with him is full redemption. (NIV)

5. **These word pictures from the Old Testament show how God views our sins once they have been forgiven. This is the result of Christ's death on the cross.**

Isaiah 43:25 I—yes, I alone—will blot out your sins for my own sake and will never think of them again. (NLT)

Psalm 32:1 How blessed is he whose transgression is forgiven, whose sin is covered! How blessed is the man to whom the Lord does not impute iniquity, and in whose spirit there is no deceit! (NASB)

Psalm 103:12 As far as the east is from the west, so far has He removed our transgressions from us. (NASB)

Isaiah 44:22 I have wiped out your transgressions like a thick cloud and your sins like a heavy mist. (NASB)

Isaiah 1:18 Come now, let us reason together, says the LORD: though your sins are like scarlet, they shall be as white as snow; though they are red like crimson, they shall become like wool. (ESV)

Isaiah 38:17 Behold, it was for my welfare that I had great bitterness; but in love you have delivered my life from the pit of destruction, for you have cast all my sins behind your back. (ESV)

Micah 7:19 He will again have compassion on us; he will tread our iniquities underfoot. You will cast all our sins into the depths of the sea. (ESV)

Psalm 51:7; see also Hebrews 8:12

6. **Nowhere in Scripture is it taught that we are to forgive ourselves. We must accept what we have done and take steps to make it**

right, but our sin was against God. Christ paid the price for all our sins and offers forgiveness. Only Jesus can forgive us.

Practical Steps

- Hold each other accountable to make sure sin is renounced and not repeated. Make restoration where needed.
- Study together as a couple Psalms 32 and 51. Make a list of what forgiveness does.
- Carefully consider together the related topic "Forgiving Each Other."
- Reflect on Christ's forgiveness. Read the crucifixion account in all four Gospels. Write down details on how forgiveness was accomplished.
- Write out on a card what God does with forgiven sin (#4 above). Read it when you are discouraged.
- Honor God by believing the truth of his forgiveness. When doubts arise, realize they come from the enemy.
- Strengthen your marriage by consistently supporting each other in accepting God's forgiveness.

Resources

- *Accepting God's Forgiveness* (booklet). C. John Miller. New Growth.
- *After You've Blown It: Reconnecting with God and Others*. Erwin Lutzer. Multnomah.
- "The Faithfulness of God" in *God as He Longs for You to See Him*. Chip Ingram. Baker.
- *The Knowledge of the Holy*. A. W. Tozer. HarperCollins.
- *What's So Amazing About Grace?* Philip Yancey. Zondervan.

Relational Needs

In marriage, a man and woman are joined in a covenant relationship, working to accomplish common goals and desiring to achieve unity of purpose. Hopefully, Christlike qualities are being mutually expressed, with each person interested in and working for the good of the other. The following topics consider relational needs.

Roles in Marriage

See also **Marriage in the Beginning**

With ever-increasing pressures from our secular world, roles in marriage are always a hot-button issue. As never before, clarity of scriptural teaching and a firm stand on the authority of God's Word is crucial. The authors would highly recommend *The Meaning of Marriage* by Timothy and Kathy Keller for a careful analysis of this topic. They make an especially strong appeal for an understanding and implementation of biblical roles.

1. **Remember that God designed us and knows what works. Marriage operates best when his plan is followed.**

Husband—loving leader

Colossians 3:19 Husbands, love your wives, and do not be harsh with them. (ESV)

1 Corinthians 7:2 But because of the temptation to sexual immorality, each man should have his own wife and each woman her own husband. (ESV)

Ephesians 5:25–33 Husbands, love your wives, just as Christ also loved the church and gave Himself for her, that He might sanctify and cleanse her with the washing of water by the word, that He might present her to Himself a glorious church, not having spot or wrinkle or any such thing, but that she should be holy and without blemish. So husbands ought to love their own wives as their own bodies; he who loves his wife loves himself. For no one ever hated his own flesh, but nourishes and cherishes it, just as the Lord does the church. For we are members of His body, of His flesh and of His bones. "For this reason a man shall leave his father and mother and be joined to his wife, and the two shall become one flesh." This is a great mystery, but I speak concerning Christ and the church. Nevertheless let each one of you in particular so love his own wife as himself, and let the wife see that she respects her husband. (NKJV)

Wife—respectful completer

Ephesians 5:22–24 Wives, submit to your own husbands, as to the Lord. For the husband is head of the wife, as also Christ is head of the church; and He is the Savior of the body. Therefore, just as the church is subject to Christ, so let the wives be to their own husbands in everything. (NKJV)

1 Peter 3:5–6 For this is the way the holy women of the past who put their hope in God used to adorn themselves. They submitted themselves to their own husbands, like Sarah, who obeyed Abraham and called him her lord. You are her daughters if you do what is right and do not give way to fear. (NIV)

Proverbs 31:10–11 A wife of noble character who can find? She is worth far more than rubies. Her husband has full confidence in her and lacks nothing of value. (NIV)

Proverbs 19:13–14 A foolish child is a father's ruin, and a quarrelsome wife is like the constant dripping of a leaky roof. Houses and wealth are inherited from parents, but a prudent wife is from the Lord. (NIV)

2. **Submission is mutual; it is for all believers. Husbands and wives should submit to the needs of each other.**

Ephesians 5:21 Submit to one another out of reverence for Christ. (NIV)

Philippians 2:3–4

3. **When a wife submits to her husband in response to his loving leadership, it is not difficult.**

Ephesians 5:25, 28–29 Husbands, love your wives, just as Christ loved the church and gave himself up for her. . . . In this same way, husbands ought to love their wives as their own bodies. He who loves his wife loves himself. After all, no one ever hated their own body, but they feed and care for their body, just as Christ does the church. (NIV)

4. **Submitting to God has priority. If a spouse is asked to do something against God's Word, we must choose to obey God. One spouse should never ask the other to commit sin, and both must say "no" to sin if pressured.**

   Acts 5:29 But Peter and the apostles answered, "We must obey God rather than men." (NASB)

   Ephesians 6:10, 13 Finally, be strong in the Lord and in the strength of his might. . . . Therefore take up the whole armor of God, that you may be able to withstand in the evil day, and having done all, to stand firm. (ESV)

   James 4:7–8; 1 Peter 5:8–9

5. **Leaving parents and becoming committed to your spouse must be in place for a marriage to function as God designed.**

   Matthew 19:4–5 Have you not read that he who created them from the beginning made them male and female, and said, "Therefore a man shall leave his father and his mother and hold fast to his wife, and the two shall become one flesh?" (ESV) (Emphasis is on the husband, but the wise wife would apply it to herself as well.)

   Genesis 2:22–24; Ephesians 5:31

Practical Steps

- Practice a team concept, each working to make the marriage succeed, with each person following God's plan.
- Plan marriage responsibilities together according to which of you is best at a specific task (while maintaining biblical roles).
- "Leaving your parents" has many aspects—physical, emotional, financial, etc. Make sure you are both committed to this concept and make your new home your priority.
- Study Wayne Mack's list of what submission is and is not in *Strengthening Your Marriage*.
- Write out together your goals for how you want your marriage to honor God.

Resources

- *The Complete Husband*. Lou Priolo. Calvary Press.
- *Designed for Joy: How the Gospel Impacts Men and Women, Identity and Practice*. Jonathan Parnell and Owen Strachan. Crossway.
- *The Excellent Wife*. Martha Peace. Focus.
- *Helper by Design: God's Perfect Plan for Women in Marriage*. Elyse Fitzpatrick. Moody.
- *Lasting Love*. Alistair Begg. Moody.
- *The Meaning of Marriage*. Tim and Kathy Keller. Hodder & Stoughton.

Communication

See also **Building Up (Each Other), Conflict, Putting Up (with Each Other), Self-Control**

Studies have shown that we communicate about 70 percent through body language, 20 percent through tone, and just 10 percent through actual words. The tongue can encourage, but it can also destroy. In a good marriage, godly communication habits, including body language and tone, are essential. Loving and kind speech and the ability to listen carefully and patiently are marks of a wise husband and wife.

1. **Key questions from Proverbs:**

   Are you able to think before you speak?

   Proverbs 29:20 There is more hope for a fool than for someone who speaks without thinking. (NLT)

   Are you able to control your temper?

   Proverbs 29:11 Fools give full vent to their rage, but the wise bring calm in the end. (NIV)

   Can you respond to others gently and without harshness?

   Proverbs 15:1 A soft answer turns away wrath, but a harsh word stirs up anger. (ESV)

   Are you able to control the quantity of talking you do?

   Proverbs 10:19 When words are many, transgression is not lacking, but whoever restrains his lips is prudent. (ESV)

   Are you able to speak patiently and softly?

   Proverbs 25:15 Patience can persuade a prince, and soft speech can break bones. (NLT)

   Do you listen fully to a problem before you speak?

   Proverbs 18:13 If one gives an answer before he hears, it is his folly and shame. (ESV)

   Are you able to be considerate and healing as you speak?

Proverbs 12:18 There is one whose rash words are like sword thrusts, but the tongue of the wise brings healing. (ESV)

Proverbs 16:24 Gracious words are like a honeycomb, sweetness to the soul and health to the body. (ESV)

Are you able to respond to the sins of others with love and without gossip?

Proverbs 17:9 Love prospers when a fault is forgiven, but dwelling on it separates close friends. (NLT)

Proverbs 20:19

Are you able to resist exaggerating or telling lies?

Proverbs 12:19 Truthful words stand the test of time, but lies are soon exposed. (NLT)

Are you able to avoid worldly and empty chatter?

Proverbs 13:3 Whoever guards his mouth preserves his life; he who opens wide his lips comes to ruin. (ESV)

2. **Consider and apply these cautions from David.**

Psalm 19:14 Let the words of my mouth and the meditation of my heart be acceptable in your sight, O Lord, my rock and my redeemer. (ESV)

Psalm 141:3 Set a guard, O Lord, over my mouth; keep watch over the door of my lips! (ESV)

3. **Speech can either grieve or please the Holy Spirit.**

Ephesians 4:29–30 Do not let any unwholesome talk come out of your mouths, but only what is helpful for building others up according to their needs, that it may benefit those who listen. And do not grieve the Holy Spirit of God, with whom you were sealed for the day of redemption. (NIV)

Ephesians 5:4

4. **Consider carefully this summary of the tongue's negative potential.**

James 3:5–10 So also the tongue is a small member, yet it boasts of great things. How great a forest is set ablaze by such a small fire! And the tongue is a fire, a world of unrighteousness. The tongue is set among our members, staining the whole body, setting on fire the entire course of life, and set on fire by hell. For every kind of beast and bird, of reptile and sea creature, can be tamed and has been tamed by mankind, but no human being can tame the tongue. It is a restless evil, full of deadly poison. With it we bless our Lord and Father, and with it we curse people who are made in the likeness of God. From the same mouth come blessing and cursing. My brothers, these things ought not to be so. (ESV)

5. **As creation gives glory to God, so should our speech.**

 Psalm 19:1–4 The heavens declare the glory of God; the skies proclaim the work of his hands. Day after day they pour forth speech; night after night they reveal knowledge. They have no speech, they use no words; no sound is heard from them. Yet their voice goes out into all the earth, their words to the ends of the world. (NIV)

 Colossians 3:17 And whatever you do, in word or deed, do everything in the name of the Lord Jesus, giving thanks to God the Father through him. (ESV)

6. **Careless words are dangerous.**

 Matthew 12:36–37 I tell you, on the day of judgment people will give account for every careless word they speak, for by your words you will be justified, and by your words you will be condemned. (ESV)

Practical Steps

- Husbands especially are notorious for not listening well to their wives. Practice careful listening. Use the McDonalds method (repeating your order back to you) and repeat back to your spouse what she has just stated. This will help ensure careful listening.
- Be sure to give eye contact when you speak and when you listen.
- Both spouses need to evaluate speech habits from your early home life. Are there good things to model? Patterns to correct? Words or "sayings" you need to omit?

- Practice not using speech to accuse others, especially your spouse.
- Be aware of your body language/nonverbal communication habits (rolling eyes, crossing arms, avoiding eye contact, etc.).
- If you are overly talkative because of nervousness, evaluate if that is caused by fear of others or insecurity. Why would that be?

Resources

- *Can We Talk? The Art of Relationship Building* (booklet). Rob Green. New Growth.
- *Communication and Conflict Resolution* (booklet). Stuart Scott. Focus.
- *War of Words*. Paul Tripp. P&R.
- *Your Family God's Way*. Wayne Mack. P&R.

Conflict

See also **Anger, Communication, Forgiving Each Other, Self-Control**

Each person approaches marriage with his or her own desires, dreams, goals, and expectations. Backgrounds can reflect different attitudes, beliefs, and behaviors. So there is no surprise when disagreements come. A wise spouse realizes that not everything needs to be agreed upon, yet some issues are important enough to seek a careful solution.

1. **The "one another" passages of Scripture guide believers to properly relate to each other. Couples need to apply these principles to help resolve conflicts.**

   Romans 12:10 Love each other with genuine affection, and take delight in honoring each other. (NLT)

   Romans 14:13 Therefore let us stop passing judgment on one another. Instead, make up your mind not to put any stumbling block or obstacle in the way of a brother or sister. (NIV)

   Romans 14:19 Let us therefore make every effort to do what leads to peace and to mutual edification. (NIV)

   Romans 15:7 Accept one another, then, just as Christ accepted you, in order to bring praise to God. (NIV)

   Romans 16:16 Greet one another with a holy kiss. (ESV)

   1 Corinthians 7:5 Do not deprive one another, except perhaps by agreement for a limited time, that you may devote yourselves to prayer; but then come together again, so that Satan may not tempt you because of your lack of self-control. (ESV) (Don't say no to sex because you aren't getting your way.)

   Ephesians 4:2–3 Be completely humble and gentle; be patient, bearing with one another in love. Make every effort to keep the unity of the Spirit through the bond of peace. (NIV)

Ephesians 4:32 Be kind and compassionate to one another, forgiving each other, just as in Christ God forgave you. (NIV)

Ephesians 5:21 Submit to one another out of reverence for Christ. (NIV)

Philippians 2:3–4 Do nothing out of selfish ambition or vain conceit. Rather, in humility value others above yourselves, not looking to your own interests but each of you to the interests of the others. (NIV)

Colossians 3:9 Don't lie to each other, for you have stripped off your old sinful nature and all its wicked deeds. (NLT)

Colossians 3:13–14 Make allowance for each other's faults, and forgive anyone who offends you. Remember, the Lord forgave you, so you must forgive others. Above all, clothe yourselves with love, which binds us all together in perfect harmony. (NLT)

1 Thessalonians 3:12 May the Lord make your love for one another and for all people grow and overflow. (NLT)

1 Thessalonians 5:11 So encourage each other and build each other up, just as you are already doing. (NLT)

1 Thessalonians 5:15 See that no one repays anyone evil for evil, but always seek to do good to one another and to everyone. (ESV)

2. **It takes work and wisdom to keep things harmonious in marriage. Anger needs to be put away. Forgiveness is required if one spouse has hurt the other.**

Romans 12:18 If possible, so far as it depends on you, live peaceably with all. (ESV)

Proverbs 3:13, 17 Blessed is the one who finds wisdom, and the one who gets understanding. . . . Her ways are ways of pleasantness, and all her paths are peace. (ESV)

Ephesians 4:30–32 Do not grieve the Holy Spirit of God, by whom you were sealed for the day of redemption. Let all bitterness and wrath and anger and clamor and slander be put away from you, along with all malice. Be kind to one another, tenderhearted, forgiving one another, as God in Christ forgave you. (ESV)

Psalm 119:165; Proverbs 3:1–2

3. **It is wrong to seek your own way. Jesus is the great example.**

   Philippians 2:3–7 Do nothing from selfish ambition or conceit, but in humility count others more significant than yourselves. Let each of you look not only to his own interests, but also to the interests of others. Have this mind among yourselves, which is yours in Christ Jesus, who, though he was in the form of God, did not count equality with God a thing to be grasped, but emptied himself, by taking the form of a servant, being born in the likeness of men. (ESV)

4. **The words we speak and the way in which they are spoken have much to do with resolving conflict.**

   Proverbs 12:18 The words of the reckless pierce like swords, but the tongue of the wise brings healing. (NIV)

   Proverbs 15:1 A gentle answer turns away wrath, but a harsh word stirs up anger. (NIV)

   Proverbs 18:13 To answer before listening—that is folly and shame. (NIV)

   Ephesians 4:29 Let no unwholesome word proceed from your mouth, but only such a word as is good for edification according to the need of the moment, so that it will give grace to those who hear. (NASB)

   Proverbs 25:11

5. **A physical or violent response to conflict is never acceptable.**

   Proverbs 14:29 People with understanding control their anger; a hot temper shows great foolishness. (NLT)

   Proverbs 3:31 Do not envy a man of violence and do not choose any of his ways. (ESV)

   Psalm 11:5 The Lord examines both the righteous and the wicked. He hates those who love violence. (NLT)

   Psalm 139:23–24 Search me, O God, and know my heart; try me and know my anxious thoughts; and see if there be any hurtful way in me, and lead me in the everlasting way. (NASB)

Practical Steps

- Keep communicating as a couple—talk, talk, talk! If you run into struggles, ask a mature married couple to help you work through the issues.
- Don't argue over unimportant details. So she doesn't squeeze the toothpaste tube from the bottom or put the cap back on? So what? Let her have her own tube!
- Ask, "Am I convinced that I am right in this situation?" Then ask, "How important is this? Is it worth fighting over? Does it matter for eternity?"
- Don't always have to be right or have the last word.
- Be willing to take advice; ask others for their thoughts. Be willing to honestly consider your spouse's viewpoint.
- Work on saying what you say with kindness and a non-elevated emotional tone. It's not just what we say, but how we say it.
- "Breathe grace!" is a well-known biblical counseling term. Our mind-set must always be reaching out to others with understanding and God's love.

Resources

- *Can We Talk?: The Art of Relationship Building* (booklet). Rob Green. New Growth.
- *Communication and Conflict Resolution* (booklet). Stuart Scott. Focus.
- *How to Act Right When Your Spouse Acts Wrong*. Leslie Vernick. WaterBrook.
- *Life on Life, Applying the One-Another Passages of Scripture*. Ellen Castillo. Word of Hope.
- *Peacemaking for Families: A Biblical Guide to Managing Conflict in Your Home*. Ken Sande and Tom Raabe. Focus.
- *The Seven Conflicts: Resolving the Most Common Disagreements in Marriage*. Tim and Joy Downs. Moody.

Truthfulness

See also **Communication, Conflict, Heart Intimacy, Integrity, Selfishness, Temptation**

Truth telling is essential to making our way through life successfully. Our walk with the Lord, employment, friends, church life, and especially marriage are all majorly dependent upon honesty. Once one or both persons begin to lie, there is often no end to lie upon lie. Consequences multiply with devastating effects to husbands, wives, family, and friends. There is no other way but to tell the truth, always!

1. **Truth telling brings great blessing.**

   Psalm 15:1–2 Who may worship in your sanctuary, Lord? Who may enter your presence on your holy hill? Those who lead blameless lives and do what is right, speaking the truth from sincere hearts. (NLT)

   Psalm 24:3–4 Who may ascend the mountain of the Lord? Who may stand in his holy place? The one who has clean hands and a pure heart, who does not trust in an idol or swear by a false god. (NIV)

   Proverbs 12:19 Truthful lips endure forever, but a lying tongue lasts only a moment. (NIV)

   Proverbs 12:22 Lying lips are an abomination to the Lord, but those who deal truthfully are His delight. (NKJV)

2. **Lying brings danger, and even death. Evaluate these examples in Scripture of what not to do.**

   Genesis 12:11–20: Abraham's lie about Sarah places her and him in grave danger.

   Genesis 26:6–11: Isaac (like father, like son) lies about Rebekah in a similar situation.

Acts 5:1–11: Ananias and Sapphira pay a heavy price for lying to God.

3. **Lying is forbidden by God and detestable to him. There is no such thing as a "white lie."**

Proverbs 24:28 Be not a witness against your neighbor without cause, and do not deceive with your lips. (ESV)

Leviticus 19:11–12 You shall not steal, nor deal falsely, nor lie to one another. And you shall not swear by My name falsely, nor shall you profane the name of your God: I am the Lord. (NKJV)

Psalm 34:13 Keep your tongue from evil, and your lips from speaking deceit. (NKJV)

Proverbs 6:16–19 These six things the Lord hates, yes, seven are an abomination to Him: a proud look, a lying tongue, hands that shed innocent blood, a heart that devises wicked plans, feet that are swift in running to evil, a false witness who speaks lies, and one who sows discord among brethren. (NKJV)

Zechariah 8:17 Don't scheme against each other. Stop your love of telling lies that you swear are the truth. I hate all these things, says the Lord. (NLT)

Exodus 20:16; 23:1–2; Psalm 5:6; James 3:14–15

4. **Though lying is a part of our sin nature, our new life in Christ makes telling the truth possible.**

Psalm 51:5 For I was born a sinner—yes, from the moment my mother conceived me. (NLT)

Psalm 58:3 Even from birth the wicked go astray; from the womb they are wayward, spreading lies. (NIV)

2 Corinthians 5:17 Therefore, if anyone is in Christ, he is a new creation. The old has passed away; behold, the new has come. (ESV)

Ephesians 4:22–25 Throw off your old sinful nature and your former way of life, which is corrupted by lust and deception. Instead, let the Spirit renew your thoughts and attitudes. Put on your new nature, created to be like God—truly righteous and holy. So stop telling lies. Let us tell our neighbors the truth, for we are all parts of the same body. (NLT)

Matthew 15:19; Romans 6:12–13; Galatians 2:20; Colossians 3:9–10; 1 John 2:21

5. **Couples who lie to each other (or to anyone) face sadness and lack of trust in their marriage.**

Psalm 5:6 You will destroy those who tell lies. The Lord detests murderers and deceivers. (NLT)

Psalm 31:18 Let their lying lips be silenced, for with pride and contempt they speak arrogantly against the righteous. (NIV)

Proverbs 12:13 The wicked are trapped by their own words, but honest people get themselves out of trouble. (GNT)

Proverbs 25:18 Telling lies about others is as harmful as hitting them with an ax, wounding them with a sword, or shooting them with a sharp arrow. (NLT)

Deuteronomy 19:16–19; Psalm 63:11; Proverbs 19:5; James 1:2

Practical Steps

- At the very beginning of your marriage, and throughout, make a verbal, heartfelt commitment to your wife/husband to always tell the truth. The rewards will be enormous.
- If you catch yourself lying, immediate repentance and confession is the very best path.
- Keep accountable with a close friend. Permit this person to evaluate your progress often.
- Why are you tempted to lie? Evaluate the reasons—is it fear of others? Will others find out about the "real you"? Worried about losing friends? Fear of rejection? Recognize your need, and see lying as God sees it.

Resources

- *Deception: Letting Go of Lying* (booklet). Lou Priolo. P&R.
- "Half Truths and Outright Lies" in *Character That Counts*. Rod Handley. Cross Training.
- "She Needs to Trust Him Totally" in *His Needs, Her Needs*. Willard F. Harley, Jr. Revell.
- "The Truth Matters" in *Pathway to Freedom: How God's Laws Guide Our Lives*. Alistair Begg. Moody.
- "Your Struggle with Truth" in *The 10 Greatest Struggles of Your Life*. Colin S. Smith. Moody.

Loving Him—Loving Her

See also **Building Up (Each Other), Communication, Conflict, Putting Up (with Each Other)**

Love is the dynamic that binds everything else together. She wants the very best for him; he wants the very best for her. What does love look like? How do we do it? What can make it last?

1. **God's love is the model and great example for which a husband and wife should strive.**

   Jeremiah 31:3 The LORD appeared to us in the past, saying: "I have loved you with an everlasting love; I have drawn you with unfailing kindness." (NIV)
   Zephaniah 3:17 For the LORD your God is living among you. He is a mighty savior. He will take delight in you with gladness. With his love, he will calm all your fears. He will rejoice over you with joyful songs. (NLT)
   Isaiah 43:4; John 3:16; 1 John 4:10, 19

2. **The love chapter gives us much of what we need.**

   1 Corinthians 13:1–8 If I could speak all the languages of earth and of angels, but didn't love others, I would only be a noisy gong or a clanging cymbal. If I had the gift of prophecy, and if I understood all of God's secret plans and possessed all knowledge, and if I had such faith that I could move mountains, but didn't love others, I would be nothing. If I gave everything I have to the poor and even sacrificed my body, I could boast about it; but if I didn't love others, I would have gained nothing. Love is patient and kind. Love is not jealous or boastful or proud or rude. It does not demand its own way. It is not irritable, and it keeps no record of being wronged. It does not rejoice about injustice but rejoices whenever the truth wins out. Love never gives up, never loses faith, is always hopeful, and endures through every circumstance. . . . But love will last forever! (NLT)

3. **Husbands are to love their wives as Christ loves his church and with the same intensity as they love themselves.**

   Ephesians 5:25–29, 33 Husbands, love your wives, just as Christ loved the church and gave himself up for her to make her holy, cleansing her by the washing with water through the word, and to present her to himself as a radiant church, without stain or wrinkle or any other blemish, but holy and blameless. In this same way, husbands ought to love their wives as their own bodies. He who loves his wife loves himself. After all, no one ever hated their own body, but they feed and care for their body, just as Christ does the church. . . . However, each one of you also must love his wife as he loves himself, and the wife must respect her husband. (NIV)

   Galatians 5:13 Through love serve one another. (ESV) (A broad command for every Christian, in the context of life lived depending on the Spirit.)

   Colossians 3:19; 1 Peter 3:7

4. **Wives are to give the gift of love and respect.**

   Titus 2:4 These older women must train the younger women to love their husbands and their children. (NLT)

   Ephesians 5:22–24 For wives, this means submit to your husbands as to the Lord. For a husband is the head of his wife as Christ is the head of the church. He is the Savior of his body, the church. As the church submits to Christ, so you wives should submit to your husbands in everything. (NLT)

   Proverbs 31:10–31

5. **It can't be done on our own. We must depend on the Holy Spirit, letting him have full control.**

   Ephesians 5:18 Don't be drunk with wine, because that will ruin your life. Instead, be filled with the Holy Spirit. (NLT) (Wine is a controlling substance and is representative of whatever in our lives is a substitute for God in control; the filling of the Spirit means he is in control.)

Galatians 5:16, 22–23 But I say, walk by the Spirit, and you will not gratify the desires of the flesh. . . . But the fruit of the Spirit is love, joy, peace, patience, kindness, goodness, faithfulness, gentleness, self-control; against such things there is no law. (ESV) (See entire paragraph.)

Practical Steps

- Find out what says "love" to your spouse. (Remember, it may be more meaningful to clean the kitchen than to buy a gift, etc.)
- The more love you give, the more love you have to give. It is never used up.
- Remember that love is a choice, not an emotion. It can have emotional qualities, but those are not the basis for the love.
- If (when) difficult times come, remember your covenant commitment and choose to love.
- Remind your spouse often of your love by saying it—"I love you." Just stating it while dating or at your wedding is not sufficient. Be lavish.

Resources

- *Family Man, Family Leader.* Philip Lancaster. Vision Forum.
- *The Five Love Languages: The Secret to Love that Lasts.* Gary Chapman. Northfield Publishers.
- *Life on Life, Applying the One-Another Passages of Scripture.* Ellen Castillo. Word of Hope.
- "The Love of God Is the Pacesetter for Marriage" in *Marriage God's Way.* Henry Brandt. B&H.
- *Strengthening Your Marriage* (workbook format). Wayne Mack. P&R.

Putting Up (with Each Other)

See also **Conflict, Communication, Disappointment, Failure, Selfishness, Self-Worth**

An important need in marriage is to acknowledge and respect differences in personality and background. Each person will bring to the marriage different styles for accomplishing goals in a daily routine. No one is perfect; everyone makes mistakes. This will necessitate acceptance and adjustments in a loving and enduring relationship. Each needs to be willing to "put up" with the other. "Don't sweat the little stuff" is a good basic rule.

1. **These relational commands and principles are for every believer. Consider the benefit to your marriage as you and your spouse carefully apply them to your lives.**

   Colossians 3:12–14 Put on then, as God's chosen ones, holy and beloved, compassionate hearts, kindness, humility, meekness, and patience, bearing with one another and, if one has a complaint against another, forgiving each other; as the Lord has forgiven you, so you also must forgive. And above all these put on love, which binds everything together in perfect harmony. (ESV)

   Ephesians 4:1–3 I therefore, a prisoner for the Lord, urge you to walk in a manner worthy of the calling to which you have been called, with all humility and gentleness, with patience, bearing with one another in love, eager to maintain the unity of the Spirit in the bond of peace. (ESV)

   Ephesians 4:32 Be kind to one another, tenderhearted, forgiving one another, as God in Christ forgave you. (ESV)

   Ephesians 5:15–21; Philippians 2:2–4

2. **Consider how love should be expressed. Evaluate your relationship with your spouse. How close are you to matching up to this standard?**

   1 Corinthians 13:4–8 Love is patient and kind; love does not envy or boast; it is not arrogant or rude. It does not insist on its own way; it is not irritable or resentful; it does not rejoice at wrongdoing, but rejoices with the truth. Love bears all things, believes all things, hopes all things, endures all things. Love never ends. (ESV)

3. **Essential to "putting up with each other" are the words we speak.**

   Proverbs 18:13 If one gives an answer before he hears, it is his folly and shame. (ESV)

   Proverbs 19:11 Good sense makes one slow to anger, and it is his glory to overlook an offense. (ESV)

   Proverbs 17:9 Whoever covers an offense seeks love, but he who repeats a matter separates close friends. (ESV)

   Proverbs 12:18 There is one whose rash words are like sword thrusts, but the tongue of the wise brings healing. (ESV)

Practical Steps

- A key component for "putting up" is patience with the other's mistakes or "just not getting it" deficiencies. Patience is kindness in action!
- Communicate openly about issues that seem to separate you. Make sure you are being kind, but truthful.
- Ask, what do these differences matter in the big picture for your marriage, or even for eternity? Write this question on a card and keep it close.
- Work on having an open mind to other ways of doing things.
- Forgiveness is essential if your spouse has demanded his or her way in the decision made.
- Work it out; talk it out; relax; breathe grace!

Resources

- *Life on Life, Applying the One-Another Passages of Scripture.* Ellen Castillo. Word of Hope.
- *Peacemaking for Families: A Biblical Guide to Managing Conflict in Your Home.* Ken Sande and Tom Raabe. Focus.
- *What Did You Expect? Redeeming the Realities of Marriage.* Paul Tripp. Crossway.
- *When Sinners Say "I Do."* Dave Harvey. Shepherd.

Building Up (Each Other)

See also **Abuse, Communication, Conflict, Putting Up (with Each Other)**

"Building" is a metaphor used frequently in Scripture and fits very well into creating a home that glorifies God. Building up your spouse, not tearing down, is an essential component for a good marriage. Building up will give your spouse "wings," not burdens.

1. **Paul's plan for his ministry was for building up people, not tearing them down. The principle applies to all relationships.**

   2 Corinthians 13:10 This is why I write these things when I am absent, that when I come I may not have to be harsh in my use of authority—the authority the Lord gave me for building you up, not for tearing you down. (NIV)

2. **God uses gifted people to build up his Church. The basic tool for this building is love. This also should be the goal in every relationship.**

   Ephesians 4:11–13 So Christ himself gave the apostles, the prophets, the evangelists, the pastors and teachers, to equip his people for works of service, so that the body of Christ may be built up until we all reach unity in the faith and in the knowledge of the Son of God and become mature, attaining to the whole measure of the fullness of Christ. (NIV)

   Ephesians 4:16 From him the whole body, joined and held together by every supporting ligament, grows and builds itself up in love, as each part does its work. (NIV)

   Jude 20

3. **God must be at the center of building our home.**

Psalm 127:1–2 Unless the Lord builds the house, those who build it labor in vain. Unless the Lord watches over the city, the watchman stays awake in vain. It is in vain that you rise up early and go late to rest, eating the bread of anxious toil; for he gives to his beloved sleep. (ESV)

Isaiah 57:14–15 And it shall be said, "Build up, build up, prepare the way, remove every obstruction from my people's way." For thus says the One who is high and lifted up, who inhabits eternity, whose name is Holy: "I dwell in the high and holy place, and also with him who is of a contrite and lowly spirit." (ESV)

4. **People helping people, spouses helping each other, is God's plan.**

Proverbs 14:1 The wise woman builds her house, but with her own hands the foolish one tears hers down. (NIV) (This would apply to both spouses.)

Romans 15:1–2 We who are strong must be considerate of those who are sensitive about things like this. We must not just please ourselves. We should help others do what is right and build them up in the Lord. (NLT)

Ephesians 4:29 Let everything you say be good and helpful, so that your words will be an encouragement to those who hear them. (NLT)

Practical Steps

- Totally commit to never putting each other down, alone or in public—marriages need to be a safe haven for acceptance.
- Ask your spouse about their dreams, goals, and ambitions. Plan how you can support these coming true.
- Make specific plans to encourage your spouse, based on current areas of struggle. Create solutions to overcome and encourage.
- Know and empathize with your spouse's fears. Take the time together to write out detailed pros and cons for a situation, and examine remedies for it as well.

- Each must be consistently reading the Word of God. Write Deuteronomy 32:46–47 on a card and keep it close at hand as a reminder of the importance of the Word in your lives.

Resources

- *His Needs, Her Needs.* Willard F. Harley, Jr. Revell.
- *Lasting Love.* Alistair Begg. Moody.
- *The Meaning of Marriage.* Tim and Kathy Keller. Hodder & Stoughton.

Forgiving Each Other

See also **Anger, Disappointment, Failure, Forgiveness from God**

Hearing the words "I forgive you!" will provide the best of moments for any marriage. Oh, the relief and release from the pain and the guilt! Healing, renewed trust, and restoration will perhaps take longer, but what a huge step in the right direction.

1. **God's offer of forgiveness to anyone who asks is a great example to couples going through a time when one or the other (perhaps both) has sinned.**

   Psalm 130:3–4 LORD, if you kept a record of our sins, who, O Lord, could ever survive? But you offer forgiveness, that we might learn to fear you. (NLT)

   Micah 7:18–19 Where is another God like you, who pardons the guilt of the remnant, overlooking the sins of his special people? You will not stay angry with your people forever, because you delight in showing unfailing love. Once again you will have compassion on us. You will trample our sins under your feet and throw them into the depths of the ocean! (NLT)

   Psalm 30:5 For his anger lasts only a moment, but his favor lasts a lifetime! Weeping may last through the night, but joy comes with the morning. (NLT)

   Luke 23:34 And Jesus said, "Father, forgive them, for they know not what they do." (ESV)

2. **Though forgiving our spouse can be difficult, there is no other option. Forgiving is a step of obedience to God.**

   Colossians 3:12–14 Put on then, as God's chosen ones, holy and beloved, compassionate hearts, kindness, humility, meekness, and patience, bearing with one another and, if one has a complaint against another, forgiving each other; as the Lord has forgiven you, so you also must forgive. And above all these put on love, which binds everything together in perfect harmony. (ESV)

Ephesians 4:32 Be kind and compassionate to one another, forgiving each other, just as in Christ God forgave you. (NIV)

Matthew 6:12–13 And forgive us our sins, as we have forgiven those who sin against us. And don't let us yield to temptation, but rescue us from the evil one. (NLT)

3. **Keeping a record of how many times you have forgiven could hurt the restoration and healing process. It is not our place to do so.**

Luke 17:3–4 Pay attention to yourselves! If your brother sins, rebuke him, and if he repents, forgive him, and if he sins against you seven times in the day, and turns to you seven times, saying, "I repent," you must forgive him. (ESV)

Matthew 18:21–22 Then Peter came up and said to him, "Lord, how often will my brother sin against me, and I forgive him? As many as seven times?" Jesus said to him, "I do not say to you seven times, but seventy-seven times." (ESV)

Philippians 4:8 Finally, brothers and sisters, whatever is true, whatever is noble, whatever is right, whatever is pure, whatever is lovely, whatever is admirable—if anything is excellent or praiseworthy—think about such things. (NIV)

Practical Steps

- Contemplate: what would it be like if God did not forgive me? Does that change my heart for forgiving my spouse?
- When a past wrong comes to mind, work on putting it aside and not holding it against the person. Remember—it is forgiven. Commit to not bringing it up again.
- Moving on past the offense is crucial to the relationship. Take all steps necessary to do so.
- We must understand that forgiveness does not guarantee forgetting. Patience with your spouse in this area is necessary.

Resources

- *Choosing Forgiveness.* Nancy Leigh DeMoss. Moody.
- *I Should Forgive, But. . . : Finding Release from the Bondage of Anger and Bitterness.* Chuck Lynch. Word.
- *Love Life for Every Married Couple: How to Fall in Love, Stay in Love, Rekindle Your Love.* Ed Wheat. Zondervan.
- *Moving On: Beyond Forgive and Forget.* Ruth Ann Batstone. New Growth.
- *Unpacking Forgiveness.* Chris Brauns. Crossway.

Sexual Intimacy

See also **Cohabitation, Flirting, Heart Intimacy, Temptation**

In a sex-obsessed environment it's easy to forget that male and female, marriage and sex, are a part of God's creation. Our moral slide as a society is moving more quickly than ever away from the absolutes of biblical morality. Satan's counterfeits are everywhere. More than ever before, believers need a solid commitment to a biblical sexuality designed and ordered by God.

1. **Sexual intercourse is a part of God's original design and is for our good. Creation as male and female was his idea.**

   Matthew 19:4 He answered, "Have you not read that he who created them from the beginning made them male and female." (ESV)

   Genesis 1:27; Hebrews 13:4

2. **Sex is the glue that binds a husband and wife together as one flesh. This oneness concept also applies to many other aspects of marriage.**

   Genesis 2:23–25 The man said, "This is now bone of my bones and flesh of my flesh; she shall be called 'woman,' for she was taken out of man." That is why a man leaves his father and mother and is united to his wife, and they become one flesh. Adam and his wife were both naked, and they felt no shame. (NIV)

   Matthew 19:5–6 Therefore a man shall leave his father and his mother and hold fast to his wife, and the two shall become one flesh. So they are no longer two but one flesh. What therefore God has joined together, let not man separate. (ESV)

3. **There are three biblical reasons for sexual intimacy in marriage.**

Children

Genesis 9:1, 7 And God blessed Noah and his sons and said to them, "Be fruitful and multiply and fill the earth. . . . And you, be fruitful and multiply, increase greatly on the earth and multiply in it." (ESV)

Psalm 127:3 Behold, children are a heritage from the Lord, the fruit of the womb a reward. (ESV)

Enjoyment

Proverbs 5:18–19 Let your fountain be blessed, and rejoice in the wife of your youth, a lovely deer, a graceful doe. Let her breasts fill you at all times with delight; be intoxicated always in her love. (ESV)

Purity (Avoiding Immorality)

1 Corinthians 7:2 But because of the temptation to sexual immorality, each man should have his own wife and each woman her own husband. (ESV)

1 Corinthians 6:18–20

4. **The husband and wife are responsible for giving sexual satisfaction to each other.**

1 Corinthians 7:3–4 The husband should give to his wife her conjugal rights, and likewise the wife to her husband. For the wife does not have authority over her own body, but the husband does. Likewise the husband does not have authority over his own body, but the wife does. (ESV)

5. **Having sex on a frequent and consistent basis is essential. Otherwise temptation could be a problem. And remember, sex is not a bargaining tool!**

Proverbs 5:19 Let her breasts fill you at all times with delight; be intoxicated always in her love. (ESV) (Note the "all times" and "always.")

1 Corinthians 7:5 Do not deprive one another, except perhaps by agreement for a limited time, that you may devote yourselves to prayer; but then come together again, so that Satan may not tempt you because of your lack of self-control. (ESV)

6. **Sexual intimacy is seen as incredible and beautiful and that which brings delight to both partners.**

Song of Solomon 7:1–9 How beautiful your sandaled feet, O prince's daughter! Your graceful legs are like jewels, the work of an artist's hands. Your navel is a rounded goblet that never lacks blended wine. Your waist is a mound of wheat encircled by lilies. Your breasts are like two fawns, like twin fawns of a gazelle. Your neck is like an ivory tower. Your eyes are the pools of Heshbon by the gate of Bath Rabbim. Your nose is like the tower of Lebanon looking toward Damascus. Your head crowns you like Mount Carmel. Your hair is like royal tapestry; the king is held captive by its tresses. How beautiful you are and how pleasing, my love, with your delights! Your stature is like that of the palm, and your breasts like clusters of fruit. I said, "I will climb the palm tree; I will take hold of its fruit." May your breasts be like clusters of grapes on the vine, the fragrance of your breath like apples, and your mouth like the best wine. (NIV)

7. **While intimacy should be a constant in the marriage, there will be times when having sex is not possible because of illness or personal crisis. Sex is never to be demanded or forced.**

1 Corinthians 13:4–7 Love is patient and kind; love does not envy or boast; it is not arrogant or rude. It does not insist on its own way; it is not irritable or resentful; it does not rejoice at wrongdoing, but rejoices with the truth. Love bears all things, believes all things, hopes all things, endures all things. (ESV)

Philippians 2:3–4 Do nothing from selfishness or empty conceit, but with humility of mind regard one another as more important than yourselves; do not merely look out for your own personal interests, but also for the interests of others. (NASB)

Practical Steps

- Be thankful for God's unique creation of humans: 1) Most mammals mate only when the female is in heat (ovulating) but humans mate quite often; 2) Humans are the only mammals that mate face to face! God's plan was intimacy.
- Read Song of Solomon out loud in a modern translation—each spouse reading a part. What is God's plan for intimacy?
- Submission in marriage does not mean sex on demand or forced.
- Each spouse needs to communicate freely what is pleasing to them (or what is not). Enjoy what is mutually pleasurable. Never do anything that causes pain.
- Since men are extremely sensitive to the visual image of the female body, a wife needs to be open to meeting this need for her husband. See Song of Solomon 7:6–8.
- Plan times away from home as a couple. Take weekend getaways.
- If a husband experiences physical problems or a wife experiences pain, consult with your physician.
- Sexual intimacy is a "barometer" within marriage. Be sure to practice good communication, forgiveness, and resolving of conflicts and issues of handling of children.
- Understand that since intimacy is God's design, he gives no timetable for it ending. Sexual activity should continue throughout one's married life.

Resources

- *His Needs, Her Needs*. Willard F. Harley Jr. Revell.
- *Intended for Pleasure*. Ed Wheat. Revell.
- *Intimate Issues: Conversations Woman to Woman—21 Questions Christian Women Ask about Sex*. Linda Dillow. WaterBrook.
- *Love, Sex, and Lasting Relationships*. Chip Ingram. Baker.
- "Sex, Romance and the Glory of God" in *Sex and the Supremacy of Christ*. John Piper and Justin Taylor. Crossway.
- "Sexuality" in *Culture Shock*. Chip Ingram. Baker.

Heart Intimacy

See also **Forgiving Each Other, Integrity, Loving Him—Loving Her, Sexual Intimacy, Truthfulness**

Scriptural concepts that promote intimacy and longevity in marriage:

1. **Practicing integrity—each knowing the other desires to live above reproach**

   Proverbs 28:6 Better is a poor man who walks in his integrity than a rich man who is crooked in his ways. (ESV)

   Psalm 15:1–3 O Lord, who may abide in Your tent? Who may dwell on Your holy hill? He who walks with integrity, and works righteousness, and speaks truth in his heart. He does not slander with his tongue, nor does evil to his neighbor, nor takes up a reproach against his friend. (NASB)

   Proverbs 2:7 He stores up sound wisdom for the upright; He is a shield to those who walk in integrity. (NASB)

2. **Practicing honesty—openness, no hiding, living in safety and freedom**

   Ephesians 4:25 No more lying, then! Each of you must tell the truth to the other believer, because we are all members together in the body of Christ. (GNT)

   Proverbs 6:16–19 There are seven things that the Lord hates and cannot tolerate: A proud look, a lying tongue, hands that kill innocent people, a mind that thinks up wicked plans, feet that hurry off to do evil, a witness who tells one lie after another, and someone who stirs up trouble among friends. (GNT)

3. **Knowing what love is and is not—committed far beyond feelings alone**

1 Corinthians 13:4–7 Love is patient and kind; love does not envy or boast; it is not arrogant or rude. It does not insist on its own way; it is not irritable or resentful; it does not rejoice at wrongdoing, but rejoices with the truth. Love bears all things, believes all things, hopes all things, endures all things. (ESV)

4. **Realizing that it's not all about you—being selfless, living for the other's best**

Philippians 2:3–4 Do nothing out of selfish ambition or vain conceit. Rather, in humility value others above yourselves, not looking to your own interests but each of you to the interests of the others. (NIV)

Romans 15:2–3

5. **Listening carefully before speaking**

Proverbs 18:13 If one gives an answer before he hears, it is his folly and shame. (ESV)

James 1:19 Understand this, my dear brothers and sisters: You must all be quick to listen, slow to speak, and slow to get angry. (NLT)

6. **Speaking softly and carefully—seeking clarification if needed**

Proverbs 15:1, 4 A gentle answer deflects anger, but harsh words make tempers flare. . . . Gentle words are a tree of life; a deceitful tongue crushes the spirit. (NLT)

Proverbs 12:18 Some people make cutting remarks, but the words of the wise bring healing. (NLT)

7. **Speaking intimately and expressively—freedom to share dreams and fears**

Song of Solomon 7:1–3, 6–9 How beautiful are your sandaled feet, O queenly maiden. Your rounded thighs are like jewels, the work of a skilled craftsman. Your navel is perfectly formed like a goblet filled with mixed wine. Between your thighs lies a mound of wheat bordered with lilies. Your breasts are like two fawns, twin fawns of a gazelle. . . . Oh, how beautiful you are! How pleasing, my love, how full of delights! You are slender like a palm tree, and your breasts are like its clusters of fruit. I said, "I will climb the palm tree and take hold of its fruit." May your breasts be like grape clusters, and the fragrance of your breath like apples. May your kisses be as exciting as the best wine . . . flowing gently over lips and teeth. (NLT)

8. **Experiencing the fruit of the Spirit in one's life**

   Galatians 5:22–23 The fruit of the Spirit is love, joy, peace, patience, kindness, goodness, faithfulness, gentleness, self-control; against such things there is no law. (ESV)

9. **Understanding the differences between a man and a woman, knowing that marriage works best following God's plan**

   1 Peter 3:7 Likewise, husbands, live with your wives in an understanding way, showing honor to the woman as the weaker vessel, since they are heirs with you of the grace of life, so that your prayers may not be hindered. (ESV)

Practical Steps

- Ask your spouse how he/she really feels about your relationship. What can each be doing to improve intimacy?
- Get away for an occasional weekend without children. Plan "dates" often, all throughout your marriage.
- Pray and read your Bible with your spouse on a daily basis.
- Always work on communication. Don't permit conflicts to build—handle them biblically. Men especially need to develop the art of careful, interested listening.
- Always kiss each other goodnight. Show affection by loving touches—holding hands, arm around the other, etc.

- At the end of the day, share your happiest and saddest moments of the day to really help understand what is meaningful to your spouse.

Resources

- *Can We Talk? The Art of Relationship Building* (booklet). Rob Green. New Growth.
- *Each for the Other: Marriage as It's Meant to Be*. Bryan and Kathy Chapel. Baker.
- *Lasting Love*. Alistair Begg. Moody.
- *Love, Sex, and Lasting Relationships*. Chip Ingram. Baker.

In-Laws

See also **Communication, Conflict, Self-Control**

Getting along with in-laws can be tricky. Our usual human relationship encounters can be intensified as a new family launches from two often divergent backgrounds. Handling these new relationships scripturally is imperative.

1. **The words we say and how we say them become especially important for this in-law relationship.**

   Proverbs 15:1 A gentle answer deflects anger, but harsh words make tempers flare. (NLT)

   Proverbs 25:11 A word fitly spoken is like apples of gold in a setting of silver. (ESV)

   Proverbs 16:24 Gracious words are like a honeycomb, sweetness to the soul and health to the body. (ESV)

   James 1:19 Understand this, my dear brothers and sisters: You must all be quick to listen, slow to speak, and slow to get angry. (NLT)

2. **Sacrificial attitudes and actions must be in place. Love must prevail.**

   Philippians 2:3–6 Do nothing from selfish ambition or conceit, but in humility count others more significant than yourselves. Let each of you look not only to his own interests, but also to the interests of others. Have this mind among yourselves, which is yours in Christ Jesus, who, though he was in the form of God, did not count equality with God a thing to be grasped. (ESV)

   1 Corinthians 13:4–7 Love is patient and kind; love does not envy or boast; it is not arrogant or rude. It does not insist on its own way; it is not irritable or resentful; it does not rejoice at wrongdoing, but rejoices with the truth. Love bears all things, believes all things, hopes all things, endures all things. (ESV)

3. **When we feel sinned against, forgiveness takes priority.**

   Ephesians 4:30–32 And do not grieve the Holy Spirit of God, by whom you were sealed for the day of redemption. Let all bitterness and wrath and anger and clamor and slander be put away from you, along with all malice. Be kind to one another, tenderhearted, forgiving one another, as God in Christ forgave you. (ESV)

4. **All involved must acknowledge the leaving and cleaving teachings of Scripture. A couple must maintain their own privacy and unity.**

   Matthew 19:4–6 He answered, "Have you not read that he who created them from the beginning made them male and female, and said, 'Therefore a man shall leave his father and his mother and hold fast to his wife, and the two shall become one flesh'? So they are no longer two but one flesh. What therefore God has joined together, let not man separate." (ESV)

   Ephesians 4:1–3 I therefore, a prisoner for the Lord, urge you to walk in a manner worthy of the calling to which you have been called, with all humility and gentleness, with patience, bearing with one another in love, eager to maintain the unity of the Spirit in the bond of peace. (ESV) (The context is relationships in a church setting, but the principles here apply.)

   Genesis 2:24

5. **All involved must do their best to maintain a peaceful climate of "getting along."**

   Romans 12:17–18 Repay no one evil for evil, but give thought to do what is honorable in the sight of all. If possible, so far as it depends on you, live peaceably with all. (ESV)

   2 Timothy 2:23 But keep away from foolish and ignorant arguments; you know that they end up in quarrels. (GNT)

6. **Patience is absolutely essential.**

2 Corinthians 6:6 We prove ourselves by our purity, our understanding, our patience, our kindness, by the Holy Spirit within us, and by our sincere love. (NLT)

1 Peter 2:19 For God is pleased when, conscious of his will, you patiently endure unjust treatment. (NLT)

Colossians 3:12; 1 Thessalonians 5:14

Practical Steps

- Understand that in most families your in-laws will be different (weird)! Once you know this and accept it, life becomes much simpler. You will learn to live with it, to "build that bridge and get over it."
- It takes hard work to make it work with your in-laws, especially if they are difficult.
- Be the bridge-builder. Build relationships—write letters, emails, thank-you notes. Send pictures; make those necessary phone calls.
- Do not be threatened if your spouse compares you to his/her parents. Use it as a springboard for communication. Perhaps this can help you learn things to avoid that hurt your relationship.

Resources

- "Commitment to Build Positive In-Law Relationships" in *So You're Getting Married*. Norm Wright. Regal.
- *In-Laws: Married with Parents*. Wayne Mack. P&R.
- *The Peacemaker: A Biblical Guide to Resolving Personal Conflict*. Ken Sande. Baker.

Unbelieving Spouse

See also **Anxiety, Roles in Marriage**

Your husband or your wife doesn't know the Lord. Believing in Jesus, walking closely with him, and enjoying the fellowship of God's people is not a part of his or her life. Your greatest desire is that this much-loved spouse would come to faith. So how does that work; what can you do? What should you not do?

1. **Every believer needs to demonstrate a godly lifestyle that serves as a testimony to unbelievers, helping them see the difference Christ can make.**

   Matthew 5:16 In the same way, let your light shine before others, so that they may see your good works and give glory to your Father who is in heaven. (ESV)

   Colossians 4:5–6 Walk in wisdom toward outsiders, making the best use of the time. Let your speech always be gracious, seasoned with salt, so that you may know how you ought to answer each person. (ESV)

   1 Peter 2:12 Be careful to live properly among your unbelieving neighbors. Then even if they accuse you of doing wrong, they will see your honorable behavior, and they will give honor to God when he judges the world. (NLT)

   Titus 2:11–14; 1 Peter 1:14–16

2. **One who lives responsibly under God's grace can reach out more effectively to an unbelieving spouse. No nagging or constant subtle hints, no preaching.**

   1 Corinthians 7:12–17 Now, I will speak to the rest of you, though I do not have a direct command from the Lord. If a fellow believer has a wife who is not a believer and she is willing to continue living with him, he must not leave her. And if a believing woman has a husband who is not a believer and he is willing to continue living with her, she must not leave him. For the believing wife brings holiness to her marriage, and the believing husband brings holiness to his marriage. Otherwise, your children would not be holy, but now they are holy. (But if the husband or wife who isn't a believer insists on leaving, let them go. In such cases the believing husband or wife is no longer bound to the other, for God has called you to live in peace.) Don't you wives realize that your husbands might be saved because of you? And don't you husbands realize that your wives might be saved because of you? Each of you should continue to live in whatever situation the Lord has placed you, and remain as you were when God first called you. This is my rule for all the churches. (NLT)

1 Peter 3:1–2 Wives, in the same way submit yourselves to your own husbands so that, if any of them do not believe the word, they may be won over without words by the behavior of their wives, when they see the purity and reverence of your lives. (NIV) (Though addressed to wives, the reverse would be true for a husband with an unbelieving wife.)

Matthew 5:16; John 13:35

3. **It is heartening to know that what seems impossible to us is certainly not impossible with God.**

Jeremiah 32:17 Ah, Lord God! It is you who have made the heavens and the earth by your great power and by your outstretched arm! Nothing is too hard for you. (ESV)

Matthew 19:26 Jesus looked at them intently and said, "Humanly speaking, it is impossible. But with God everything is possible." (NLT) (The context here is evangelism, but the principle applies.)

Genesis 18:14; Job 42:2

4. **The believing spouse must live a consistent life of obedience, choosing to follow God completely, not allowing the unbeliever to compel them to sin.**

   John 14:15, 21 If you love me, you will keep my commandments. . . .Whoever has my commandments and keeps them, he it is who loves me. And he who loves me will be loved by my Father, and I will love him and manifest myself to him. (ESV)

   Deuteronomy 10:12–13, 20–21 And now, Israel, what does the Lord your God ask of you but to fear the Lord your God, to walk in obedience to him, to love him, to serve the Lord your God with all your heart and with all your soul, and to observe the Lord's commands and decrees that I am giving you today for your own good? . . . Fear the Lord your God and serve him. Hold fast to him and take your oaths in his name. He is the one you praise; he is your God, who performed for you those great and awesome wonders you saw with your own eyes. (NIV)

5. **Being married to an unbelieving husband or wife is never a reason or excuse for divorce.**

   1 Corinthians 7:12–13 But to the rest I say, not the Lord, that if any brother has a wife who is an unbeliever, and she consents to live with him, he must not divorce her. And a woman who has an unbelieving husband, and he consents to live with her, she must not send her husband away. (NASB)

Practical Steps

- Don't argue, place a guilt trip, or force discussions. Live a life of quiet example.
- Develop accountability with other strong believers who can provide wisdom and prayer support.
- Do not permit church or ministry to come between you and your spouse.
- Earnestly pray for your spouse often. Create a plan to accomplish this.

Resources

- *Beloved Unbeliever*. Jo Berry. Zondervan.
- "Counseling Women Married to Unbelievers" in *Women Helping Women*. Elyse Fitzpatrick. Harvest House.
- *Love and Respect: The Love She Most Desires; The Respect He Desperately Desires*. Emerson Eggerichs. Integrity.

Blended Family

See also **Communication, Conflict, Essential Disciplines, Handling the Past, Putting Up (with Each Other)**

In a blended family one or both spouses have been married before and children from different birth families are a part of a new household. It is often a complicated situation that takes abundant wisdom and patience from everyone involved. Primary goals would include: each person feeling understood and accepted, and each one adjusting positively to the new family experience.

1. **Reflect on these relational commands and principles as you and your new spouse work to make this a successful blending. Note that many of the descriptive words are about attitude.**

   Colossians 3:12–14 Put on then, as God's chosen ones, holy and beloved, compassionate hearts, kindness, humility, meekness, and patience, bearing with one another and, if one has a complaint against another, forgiving each other; as the Lord has forgiven you, so you also must forgive. And above all these put on love, which binds everything together in perfect harmony. (ESV)

   Ephesians 4:1–3 I therefore, a prisoner for the Lord, urge you to walk in a manner worthy of the calling to which you have been called, with all humility and gentleness, with patience, bearing with one another in love, eager to maintain the unity of the Spirit in the bond of peace. (ESV)

   Ephesians 4:32 Be kind to one another, tenderhearted, forgiving one another, as God in Christ forgave you. (ESV)

   Ephesians 5:15–21; Philippians 2:2–4

2. **Communication that includes careful listening is essential for these new relationships. The words we choose are important, but also tone and body language.**

   Proverbs 18:13 If one gives an answer before he hears, it is his folly and shame. (ESV)

   James 3:5 So also the tongue is a small member, yet it boasts of great things. How great a forest is set ablaze by such a small fire! (ESV)

   Proverbs 12:18 There is one whose rash words are like sword thrusts, but the tongue of the wise brings healing. (ESV)

   Proverbs 17:27 A truly wise person uses few words; a person with understanding is even-tempered. (NLT)

   Proverbs 10:19; 12:19; 29:11, 20

3. **Consider the many possibilities for love to be expressed. Evaluate the relationships with each family member. How close are you to matching up to the standard in 1 Corinthians 13?**

   1 Corinthians 13:4–8 Love is patient and kind; love does not envy or boast; it is not arrogant or rude. It does not insist on its own way; it is not irritable or resentful; it does not rejoice at wrongdoing, but rejoices with the truth. Love bears all things, believes all things, hopes all things, endures all things. Love never ends. (ESV)

4. **A sacrificial attitude will greatly enhance the new interactions. Placing the needs of others before ourselves will invigorate and sustain the family. Jesus provides the great example.**

   Philippians 2:2–8 Complete my joy by being of the same mind, having the same love, being in full accord and of one mind. Do nothing from selfish ambition or conceit, but in humility count others more significant than yourselves. Let each of you look not only to his own interests, but also to the interests of others. Have this mind among yourselves, which is yours in Christ Jesus, who, though he was in the form of God, did not count equality with God a thing to be grasped, but emptied himself, by taking the form of a servant, being born in the likeness of men. And being found in human form, he humbled himself by becoming obedient to the point of death, even death on a cross. (ESV)

5. **Make sure that necessary spiritual disciplines are consistently in place and actively pursued. Maintain that close walk with Christ.**

Psalm 55:17 Morning, noon, and night I cry out in my distress, and the Lord hears my voice. (NLT)

Matthew 26:41 Watch and pray that you may not enter into temptation. The spirit indeed is willing, but the flesh is weak. (ESV)

Hebrews 10:24–25 And let us consider how to stir up one another to love and good works, not neglecting to meet together, as is the habit of some, but encouraging one another, and all the more as you see the Day drawing near. (ESV)

Deuteronomy 6:6–7 And these words that I command you today shall be on your heart. You shall teach them diligently to your children, and shall talk of them when you sit in your house, and when you walk by the way, and when you lie down, and when you rise. (ESV)

Ephesians 6:10–11 Finally, be strong in the Lord and in the strength of his might. Put on the whole armor of God, that you may be able to stand against the schemes of the devil. (ESV)

Joshua 1:8; Galatians 5:16; Ephesians 5:18; 6:18

Practical Steps

- Practice frequent family meetings. Communicate openly about issues that seem to separate you. Make sure you are being kind, but truthful. Include everyone.
- Plan family activities in which each person can participate and enjoy themselves.
- Work on having an open mind to other ways of doing things.
- Forgiveness and extensive communication are essential if a family member has demanded their way in a discussion.

- Work it out; talk it out; relax; breathe grace! Unconditional love is the key!
- Be alert for bitterness and resentment. It is no longer "his kids, her kids" but "our family."

Resources

- *Peacemaking for Families: A Biblical Guide to Managing Conflict in Your Home*. Ken Sande and Tom Raabe. Focus.
- *Smart Stepfamily Marriage: Keys to Success in the Blended Family*. David Olson and Ron L. Deal. Bethany House.
- *What Did You Expect? Redeeming the Realities of Marriage*. Paul Tripp. Crossway.

Faithfulness to Each Other

Fidelity is at the top of most lists for happiness and longevity in marriage. Remaining faithful to each other is an irrevocable matter of commitment. The scriptural concept of being a "one-woman man" (1 Timothy 3:2) and conversely, a "one-man woman," means that all of your needs for relationship with the opposite sex are to be supplied through that wife/husband God has given you. Being faithful means much more than just avoiding actual sexual intercourse with someone else.

Temptation

See also **Fantasizing, Flirting, Materialism, Purity, Thought Life**

Crucial to our walking closely with Christ and to each other in marriage is resisting temptations that come. Sinful attitudes, thoughts, and activities must be avoided. Three key areas are: pressures from the world system, our own fleshly desires, and Satan's attacks.

1. **To experience temptation is not sin, but is something to be faced as a part of a sinful world. Temptation is where the battle begins.**

   James 1:14 Temptation comes from our own desires, which entice us and drag us away. (NLT)

   Romans 7:18 And I know that nothing good lives in me, that is, in my sinful nature. I want to do what is right, but I can't. (NLT)

2. **Christ's death included provision for victory over sin.**

   2 Peter 1:3–4 His divine power has given us everything we need for a godly life through our knowledge of him who called us by his own glory and goodness. Through these he has given us his very great and precious promises, so that through them you may participate in the divine nature, having escaped the corruption in the world caused by evil desires. (NIV)

3. **Since God has made provision to resist sin, we need courage and commitment to follow through, choosing to obey Him.**

   Joshua 24:14–15 So fear the Lord and serve him wholeheartedly. Put away forever the idols your ancestors worshiped when they lived beyond the Euphrates River and in Egypt. Serve the Lord alone. But if you refuse to serve the Lord, then choose today whom you will serve. Would you prefer the gods your ancestors served beyond the Euphrates? Or will it be the gods of the Amorites in whose land you now live? But as for me and my family, we will serve the LORD. (NLT)

1 Corinthians 10:13 The temptations in your life are no different from what others experience. And God is faithful. He will not allow the temptation to be more than you can stand. When you are tempted, he will show you a way out so that you can endure. (NLT)

1 John 4:4 You are from God, little children, and have overcome them; because greater is He who is in you than he who is in the world. (NASB)

Hebrews 12:1–2 Therefore, since we are surrounded by such a great cloud of witnesses, let us throw off everything that hinders and the sin that so easily entangles. And let us run with perseverance the race marked out for us, fixing our eyes on Jesus, the pioneer and perfecter of faith. (NIV)

Ephesians 6:10–18

4. **Enlisting the help of other Christian couples for accountability and support is wise.**

Galatians 6:2 Help carry one another's burdens, and in this way you will obey the law of Christ. (GNT)

Romans 15:1–2 We who are strong in the faith ought to help the weak to carry their burdens. We should not please ourselves. Instead, we should all please other believers for their own good, in order to build them up in the faith. (GNT)

5. **Couples who go without sex over a period of time risk temptation. Sex needs to be regular and often.**

1 Corinthians 7:5 Do not deprive each other of sexual relations, unless you both agree to refrain from sexual intimacy for a limited time so you can give yourselves more completely to prayer. Afterward, you should come together again so that Satan won't be able to tempt you because of your lack of self-control. (NLT)

6. **Consistent obedience to these commands regarding the Holy Spirit is crucial for resisting temptation.**

Ephesians 5:18 Do not get drunk with wine, which will only ruin you; instead, be filled with the Spirit. (GNT) (Important thought: don't let the things of this life control you, but instead, let God's Spirit be in charge.)

Galatians 5:16 But I say, walk by [depend on] the Spirit, and you will not gratify the desires of the flesh. (ESV)

Ephesians 4:30 And do not grieve the Holy Spirit of God, by whom you were sealed for the day of redemption. (ESV)

1 Thessalonians 5:19 Do not quench the Spirit. (ESV)

Practical Steps

- Often your best accountability partner is that man/woman you chose to be your spouse. Openly admit what triggers you and take steps together to avoid those areas.
- Do a scriptural study of the three enemies of the believer—the world, the flesh, and the Devil. Note how the three relate to each other and how we must be vigilant in the battle.
- Know your own weaknesses. From 1 John 2:15–17, study the three areas of temptation. List your own personal battles for each. Compare this passage to Genesis 3, where Adam and Eve sinned in these three areas.
- Remove temptations from your home, office, car, cell phone. Evaluate places you go to frequently; commit to staying away from those that lead to temptation.
- Memorize 1 Corinthians 10:13. Write it on a card to keep close at hand.

Resources

- *Christ and Your Problems* (booklet). Jay Adams. P&R.
- *How in This World Can I Be Holy?* Erwin Lutzer. Moody.

- "A Powerful Response to Temptation" in *The Hand of God: Finding His Care in all Circumstances*. Alistair Begg. Moody.
- *Temptation: Fighting the Urge* (booklet). Timothy Lane. CEF.
- *Winning the Inner War: How to Say No to a Stubborn Habit*. Erwin Lutzer. Cook.

Fantasizing

See also **Flirting, Purity, Temptation, Thought Life**

True followers of Christ want to avoid the actual, physical sin of committing adultery. Yet what we would never act on, we are often tempted to think about. Scripture is clear—imagining/fantasizing about having sex with someone other than one's spouse is sin.

1. Lust is caused by disobedience to God's Word.

Psalm 119:9, 11 How can a young person stay pure? By obeying your word. . . . I have hidden your word in my heart, that I might not sin against you. (NLT)

Mark 4:19 But the worries of this life, the deceitfulness of wealth and the desires for other things come in and choke the word, making it unfruitful. (NIV)

Ephesians 4:22 You were taught, with regard to your former way of life, to put off your old self, which is being corrupted by its deceitful desires. (NIV)

2 Timothy 4:3–4 For the time will come when people will not put up with sound doctrine. Instead, to suit their own desires, they will gather around them a great number of teachers to say what their itching ears want to hear. They will turn their ears away from the truth and turn aside to myths. (NIV)

2. We must discipline ourselves toward thinking godly thoughts.

1 Peter 1:13 Therefore, with minds that are alert and fully sober, set your hope on the grace to be brought to you when Jesus Christ is revealed at his coming. (NIV)

Philippians 4:8 And now, dear brothers and sisters, one final thing. Fix your thoughts on what is true, and honorable, and right, and pure, and lovely, and admirable. Think about things that are excellent and worthy of praise. (NLT)

2 Corinthians 10:5 We demolish arguments and every pretension that sets itself up against the knowledge of God, and we take captive every thought to make it obedient to Christ. (NIV)

3. **Thinking as God thinks should be our standard. Throw evil fantasies aside; don't go there! Stop them the second they cross your mind.**

Isaiah 55:7–8 Let the wicked forsake their ways and the unrighteous their thoughts. Let them turn to the Lord, and he will have mercy on them, and to our God, for he will freely pardon. "For my thoughts are not your thoughts, neither are your ways my ways," declares the Lord. (NIV)

Ephesians 4:22–24 You were taught, with regard to your former way of life, to put off your old self, which is being corrupted by its deceitful desires; to be made new in the attitude of your minds; and to put on the new self, created to be like God in true righteousness and holiness. (NIV)

4. **We need a commitment to not look, or to look away.**

Matthew 5:28 But I tell you that anyone who looks at a woman lustfully has already committed adultery with her in his heart. (NIV)

Proverbs 4:25–27 Let your eyes look straight ahead; fix your gaze directly before you. Give careful thought to the paths for your feet and be steadfast in all your ways. Do not turn to the right or the left; keep your foot from evil. (NIV)

Job 31:1 I made a covenant with my eyes not to look with lust at a young woman. (NLT)

Psalm 101:3

5. **With God's help, it is possible to avoid lustful thoughts.**

2 Timothy 2:22 Now flee from youthful lusts and pursue righteousness, faith, love and peace, with those who call on the Lord from a pure heart. (NASB)

Titus 2:12 It teaches us to say "No" to ungodliness and worldly passions, and to live self-controlled, upright and godly lives in this present age. (NIV)

1 Corinthians 10:13 No temptation has overtaken you that is not common to man. God is faithful, and he will not let you be tempted beyond your ability, but with the temptation he will also provide the way of escape, that you may be able to endure it. (ESV)

Romans 6:12–13 Therefore do not let sin reign in your mortal body so that you obey its lusts, and do not go on presenting the members of your body to sin as instruments of unrighteousness; but present yourselves to God as those alive from the dead, and your members as instruments of righteousness to God. (NASB)

Practical Steps

- Every person knows what starts them down the path of sinful thoughts. Recognize where that "start" is for you, and go no farther.
- Ask your spouse to verbalize how your lustful thoughts toward others are hurtful to them.
- Avoid books with graphic sexual descriptions. Monitor your movie viewing. These areas are subtle, but damaging.
- If this is a strong habit, evaluate what is feeding this thinking—places you frequent, magazines you read, etc.
- A key area for spiritual and emotional health is exercise. Set aside time and follow through.
- Do a concordance study of the hundreds of uses in the Bible of "mind," "thinking," and "thoughts" to better understand how God wants us to think.
- When tempting thoughts come, ask God to control your mind. Pray, "Lord, please remove that thought from me," or "Lord, through your Spirit, I reject that thought."

Resources

- *Changing Your Thought Patterns* (booklet). George Sanchez. NavPress.
- *How People Change*. Timothy Lane. New Growth.
- *Right Thinking in a World Gone Wrong*. John MacArthur. Harvest House.
- *Sex Is Not the Problem (Lust Is)*. Joshua Harris. Multnomah.
- *Think Before You Look*. Daniel Henderson. Living Ink.
- *You Can Change*: *God's Transforming Power for Our Sinful Behavior and Negative Emotions*. Tim Chester. Crossway.

Purity

See also **Fantasizing, Forgiveness from God, Temptation, Thought Life**

One of the fastest ways to destroy a marriage is for one or both partners to become involved with pornography. This sin has become a plague of epic proportions in our present culture. To enjoy a successful, fulfilling marriage, this sin must be resisted and defeated.

1. **Satan's plan from the beginning has been to cause doubt in the veracity of God's commands and to provide his own counterfeit alternative.**

   Genesis 3:1–5 Now the serpent was more crafty than any other beast of the field that the Lord God had made. He said to the woman, "Did God actually say, 'You shall not eat of any tree in the garden'?" And the woman said to the serpent, "We may eat of the fruit of the trees in the garden, but God said, 'You shall not eat of the fruit of the tree that is in the midst of the garden, neither shall you touch it, lest you die.'" But the serpent said to the woman, "You will not surely die. For God knows that when you eat of it your eyes will be opened, and you will be like God, knowing good and evil." (ESV)

   1 Peter 5:8–9 Be sober-minded; be watchful. Your adversary the devil prowls around like a roaring lion, seeking someone to devour. Resist him, firm in your faith. (ESV)

2. **Satan's world system is his design to replace God's plan with his own and to promote a lack of confidence in God.**

   Matthew 13:37–40 He answered, "The one who sows the good seed is the Son of Man. The field is the world, and the good seed is the sons of the kingdom. The weeds are the sons of the evil one, and the enemy who sowed them is the devil. The harvest is the end of the age, and the reapers are angels. Just as the weeds are gathered and burned with fire, so will it be at the end of the age." (ESV)

1 John 2:15–18 Do not love the world or the things in the world. If anyone loves the world, the love of the Father is not in him. For all that is in the world— the desires of the flesh and the desires of the eyes and pride in life—is not from the Father but is from the world. And the world is passing away along with its desires, but whoever does the will of God abides forever. (ESV)

John 8:44; Ephesians 6:12; 1 John 5:19

3. **God's plan is that husbands and wives find sexual satisfaction from each other only. Men especially have a visual need for their sexual satisfaction, but this must come only from one's own spouse. The same would apply to the wife as well.**

1 Corinthians 7:2–5 But since sexual immorality is occurring, each man should have sexual relations with his own wife, and each woman with her own husband. The husband should fulfill his marital duty to his wife, and likewise the wife to her husband. The wife does not have authority over her own body but yields it to her husband. In the same way, the husband does not have authority over his own body but yields it to his wife. Do not deprive each other except perhaps by mutual consent and for a time, so that you may devote yourselves to prayer. Then come together again so that Satan will not tempt you because of your lack of self-control. (NIV)

Proverbs 5:15–22 Drink water from your own cistern, running water from your own well. Should your springs overflow in the streets, your streams of water in the public squares? Let them be yours alone, never to be shared with strangers. May your fountain be blessed, and may you rejoice in the wife of your youth. A loving doe, a graceful deer—may her breasts satisfy you always, may you ever be intoxicated with her love. Why, my son, be intoxicated with another man's wife? Why embrace the bosom of a wayward woman? For your ways are in full view of the Lord, and he examines all your paths. The evil deeds of the wicked ensnare them; the cords of their sins hold them fast.

(NIV) (The context is actual sexual activity, but the application for pornography is obvious.)

4. **Viewing pornography affects the entire marriage relationship. Secrecy, lying, deception, fornication, etc. are involved.**

Luke 11:34–36 Your eye is the lamp of your body. When your eye is healthy, your whole body is full of light, but when it is bad, your body is full of darkness. Therefore be careful lest the light in you be darkness. If then your whole body is full of light, having no part dark, it will be wholly bright, as when a lamp with its rays gives you light. (ESV)

James 1:14–15 But each person is tempted when he is lured and enticed by his own desire. Then desire when it has conceived gives birth to sin, and sin when it is fully grown brings forth death. (ESV)

5. **Scripture commands that our eyes be kept from sinning.**

Job 31:1 I made a covenant with my eyes not to look with lust at a young woman. (NLT)

Psalm 101:3–4 I will not look with approval on anything that is vile. I hate what faithless people do; I will have no part in it. The perverse of heart shall be far from me; I will have nothing to do with what is evil. (NIV)

Isaiah 1:16 Wash yourselves, make yourselves clean; remove the evil of your deeds from My sight. Cease to do evil. (NASB)

Matthew 5:28

6. **It is imperative to turn from this wickedness, choosing to obey God. We cannot be close to God, or our spouse, and involved with this sin.**

1 Corinthians 6:18–20 Flee from sexual immorality. All other sins a person commits are outside the body, but whoever sins sexually, sins against their own body. Do you not know that your bodies are temples of the Holy Spirit, who is in you, whom you have received from God? You are not your own; you were bought at a price. Therefore honor God with your bodies. (NIV)

1 Thessalonians 4:3–6 It is God's will that you should be sanctified: that you should avoid sexual immorality; that each of you should learn to control your own body in a way that is holy and honorable, not in passionate lust like the pagans, who do not know God. (NIV)

Psalm 32:3–5 When I kept silent about my sin, my body wasted away through my groaning all day long. For day and night Your hand was heavy upon me; my vitality was drained away as with the fever heat of summer. I acknowledged my sin to You, and my iniquity I did not hide; I said, "I will confess my transgressions to the LORD"; and You forgave the guilt of my sin. (NASB)

Psalm 119:37 Turn my eyes from worthless things, and give me life through your word. (NLT)

Matthew 5:29 If your right eye causes you to sin, tear it out and throw it away. For it is better that you lose one of your members than that your whole body be thrown into hell. (ESV) (See context; Jesus is speaking metaphorically.)

Romans 13:14 Instead, clothe yourself with the presence of the Lord Jesus Christ. And don't let yourself think about ways to indulge your evil desires. (NLT)

Psalm 139:23–24; 1 Peter 2:24

7. **There is hope for freedom from this sin. God supports us as we make godly choices. He hears and answers our cries for help. Quitting may be difficult, but it is possible through the Holy Spirit.**

2 Chronicles 16:9 For the eyes of the LORD run to and fro throughout the whole earth, to give strong support to those whose heart is blameless toward him. (ESV)

Galatians 5:16 But I say, walk by [depend on] the Spirit, and you will not gratify the desires of the flesh. (ESV) (See also verses 16–25.)

Psalm 33:18–20 Behold, the eye of the LORD is on those who fear Him, on those who hope for His lovingkindness, to deliver their soul from death and to keep them alive in famine. Our soul waits for the LORD; He is our help and our shield. (NASB)

Psalm 34:14–18 Depart from evil and do good; seek peace and pursue it. The eyes of the LORD are toward the righteous and

His ears are open to their cry. The face of the Lord is against evildoers, to cut off the memory of them from the earth. The righteous cry, and the Lord hears and delivers them out of all their troubles. The Lord is near to the brokenhearted and saves those who are crushed in spirit. (NASB) (See entire psalm.)

Romans 6:12–14; 1 Corinthians 6:9–11; 2 Corinthians 5:17

8. **Seeking accountability from other believers is a step toward winning these battles.**

2 Timothy 2:21–22 Therefore, if anyone cleanses himself from what is dishonorable, he will be a vessel for honorable use, set apart as holy, useful to the master of the house, ready for every good work. So flee youthful passions and pursue righteousness, faith, love, and peace, along with those who call on the Lord from a pure heart. (ESV)

Galatians 6:1–2 Brothers, if anyone is caught in any transgression, you who are spiritual should restore him in a spirit of gentleness. Keep watch on yourself, lest you too be tempted. Bear one another's burdens, and so fulfill the law of Christ. (ESV)

Practical Steps

- Pornography is always wrong; God is never glorified (2 Corinthians 5:9). What is your goal?
- Often, the best accountability person is one's own wife or husband. (This may be difficult, but necessary.) Having to admit to the other that we have sinned yet again is a major deterrent to sinning. Think how hurt they will be.
- Be alert for catalogs selling their product using the female or male body. Either stop them from coming or throw them away without looking.
- Make a strong commitment to God and to each other to obey the scriptural commands regarding the Holy Spirit—to not grieve, to be controlled by, to depend on, and to not quench his conviction in your life (Ephesians 4:30; 5:18; Galatians 5:16; 1 Thessalonians 5:19).

- If you travel alone, ask that the cable TV to your hotel room be turned off.
- Have in place computer lock-outs.

Resources

- *Closing the Window: Steps to Living Porn Free*. Tim Chester. IVP.
- *Every Man's Battle: Winning the War on Sexual Temptation One Victory at a Time* (workbook available). Stephen Arterburn. WaterBrook.
- *Pornography: Slaying the Dragon*. David Powlison. P&R.
- *Think Before You Look*. Daniel Henderson. Living Ink.
- *Winning the Inner War: How to Say No to a Stubborn Habit*. Erwin Lutzer. Cook.
- *You Can Change: God's Transforming Power for Our Sinful Behavior and Negative Emotions*. Tim Chester. Crossway.

Flirting

See also **Purity, Temptation**

For the Christian husband and wife who desire to maintain a pure commitment to each other, and a good reputation with others, flirting is off base. Defined as showing an interest in someone of the opposite sex, but without serious intent, flirting is viewed by some as an innocent activity. Yet, in our sexually charged and promiscuous culture, it can have serious repercussions and can cause great hurt and trust struggles for both spouses.

Below are texts specifically addressed to husbands and others to wives. To apply the commands and principles to the opposite sex is appropriate. Godly behavior is not gender exclusive.

For Husbands

1. **Married men must be single-minded in their devotion to the one woman God has given them. Associations with other women must be pure and responsible, never provocative.**

   1 Timothy 3:2 Therefore an overseer must be above reproach, the husband of one wife. (ESV) ("Husband of one wife" in the original language means "one-woman man"—she is to be the only source of satisfaction for his masculine needs. The context is church leadership, but the application is to every man.)

   Malachi 2:14–15 But you say, "Why does he not [accept our worship]?" Because the LORD was witness between you and the wife of your youth, to whom you have been faithless, though she is your companion and your wife by covenant. . . . So guard yourselves in your spirit, and let none of you be faithless to the wife of your youth. (ESV) (The context is divorce, but an application of "being faithless" would include flirting.)

Proverbs 21:23 Whoever keeps his mouth and his tongue keeps himself out of trouble. (ESV)

Matthew 12:36–37 I tell you, on the day of judgment people will give account for every careless word they speak, for by your words you will be justified, and by your words you will be condemned. (ESV)

2. **They are to love their wives as Christ loved his church and as they love their own bodies. This precludes flirting.**

Ephesians 5:22–30

For Wives

1. **Seductive words and actions are not appropriate in the life of a godly woman.**

Proverbs 7:4–5 Say to wisdom, "You are my sister," and call insight your intimate friend, to keep you from the forbidden woman, from the adulteress with her smooth words. (ESV)

Proverbs 6:23–25 For the commandment is a lamp and the teaching a light, and the reproofs of discipline are the way of life, to preserve you from the evil woman, from the smooth tongue of the adulteress. Do not desire her beauty in your heart, and do not let her capture you with her eyelashes. (ESV)

Matthew 12:36 But I tell you that everyone will have to give account on the day of judgment for every empty word they have spoken. (NIV)

Ephesians 5:4 Let there be no filthiness nor foolish talk nor crude joking, which are out of place, but instead let there be thanksgiving. (ESV)

Proverbs 21:23

2. **Seductive women in Israel's past faced God's discipline.**

Isaiah 3:16–17 The Lord says, "The women of Zion are haughty, walking along with outstretched necks, flirting with their eyes, strutting along with swaying hips, with ornaments jingling on their ankles. Therefore the Lord will bring sores on the heads of the women of Zion; the Lord will make their scalps bald." (NIV)

3. **A godly wife maintains a godly example.**

1 Peter 3:3–6 Don't be concerned about the outward beauty of fancy hairstyles, expensive jewelry, or beautiful clothes. You should clothe yourselves instead with the beauty that comes from within, the unfading beauty of a gentle and quiet spirit, which is so precious to God. This is how the holy women of old made themselves beautiful. They put their trust in God and accepted the authority of their husbands. (NLT)

1 Peter 2:11–12 Dear friends, I warn you as "temporary residents and foreigners" to keep away from worldly desires that wage war against your very souls. Be careful to live properly among your unbelieving neighbors. Then even if they accuse you of doing wrong, they will see your honorable behavior, and they will give honor to God when he judges the world. (NLT)

In Summary

1. **Flirtatious and provocative speech and actions are to be avoided.**

Proverbs 2:16–17 So you will be delivered [by wisdom] from the forbidden woman, from the adulteress with her smooth words, who forsakes the companion of her youth and forgets the covenant of her God. (ESV)

2 Peter 2:18 They brag about themselves with empty, foolish boasting. With an appeal to twisted sexual desires, they lure back into sin those who have barely escaped from a lifestyle of deception. (NLT)

Proverbs 10:10 Whoever winks the eye causes trouble, and a babbling fool will come to ruin. (ESV)

Isaiah 3:16–17 Moreover, the Lord said, "Because the daughters of Zion are proud and walk with heads held high and seductive eyes, and go along with mincing steps and tinkle the bangles on their feet, therefore the Lord will afflict the scalp of the daughters of Zion with scabs, and the Lord will make their foreheads bare." (NASB) (These statements apply equally to men for their similar words and actions.)

2. **Flirting could have disastrous results, causing others to choose sin.**

   Matthew 18:7 Woe to the world because of the things that cause people to stumble! Such things must come, but woe to the person through whom they come! (NIV)

   Romans 14:13, 21 Therefore let us stop passing judgment on one another. Instead, make up your mind not to put any stumbling block or obstacle in the way of a brother or sister. . . . It is better not to eat meat or drink wine or to do anything else that will cause your brother or sister to fall. (NIV)

   2 Corinthians 6:3 We put no stumbling block in anyone's path, so that our ministry will not be discredited. (NIV)

   Luke 17:1

3. **Such irresponsible behavior could open our lives to Satan's attacks.**

   Proverbs 9:13–18 The woman Folly is loud; she is seductive and knows nothing. She sits at the door of her house; she takes a seat on the highest places of the town, calling to those who pass by, who are going straight on their way, "Whoever is simple, let him turn in here!" And to him who lacks sense she says, "Stolen water is sweet, and bread eaten in secret is pleasant." But he does not know that the dead are there, that her guests are in the depths of Sheol. (ESV)

   1 Peter 5:8 Be sober-minded; be watchful. Your adversary the devil prowls around like a roaring lion, seeking someone to devour. (ESV)

   2 Corinthians 11:3 But I am afraid that just as Eve was deceived by the serpent's cunning, your minds may somehow be led astray from your sincere and pure devotion to Christ. (NIV)

   Ephesians 6:11–13

Practical Steps

- Set boundaries for relationships with the opposite sex—at work, socially, and at church.
- Never be alone with a man or woman who is not your spouse (family members excluded).
- Read Proverbs 5, and in your own words describe flirting from God's point of view.
- List flirtatious actions on one side of a paper; on the other side list opposite actions. Compare and contrast. Commit to non-flirtatious behavior.
- Ask your husband or wife how they feel when you flirt with others. Ask them to forgive you and to keep you accountable.

Resources

- "Character" in *Disciplines of a Godly Man*. Kent Hughes. Crossway.
- *Emotional Purity: An Affair of the Heart*. Heather Arnel Paulsen. Crossway.
- *Loving Your Marriage Enough to Protect It*. Jerry Jenkins. Moody.
- *Not Even a Hint* (individual study guides for men and women). Shannon and Joshua Harris. Multnomah.
- *Temptation* (booklet). Timothy Lane. CCEF.

Adultery

See also **Confession, Fantasizing, Flirting, Forgiveness from God, Forgiving Each Other, Purity, Temptation**

Adultery is any sexual involvement with someone other than your spouse or who is husband/wife to someone else. It includes feelings, thoughts, touching, or intercourse. Emotional adultery (i.e., bonding with a non-spouse: friendship, communication, etc.), even when no physical boundaries are crossed, is also a danger. All of your needs for relationship with the opposite sex are to be supplied through that wife/husband God has given you. Friendship as couple to couple is perfectly acceptable, within safe boundaries.

Adultery Is Sin

1. **Nothing is clearer from Scripture. Adultery is a sin against God, with devastating and destructive consequences. Absolutely, case closed.**

   Exodus 20:14 You shall not commit adultery. (NKJV)

   Proverbs 5:20 Why should you be intoxicated, my son, with a forbidden woman and embrace the bosom of an adulteress? (ESV)

   Romans 13:9 For the commandments say, "You must not commit adultery. You must not murder. You must not steal. You must not covet." These—and other such commandments—are summed up in this one commandment: "Love your neighbor as yourself." (NLT)

   Genesis 39:9–10

2. **It is sin to desire or take what belongs to another—another man's wife, another woman's husband.**

   Exodus 20:15, 17 You shall not steal. . . . You shall not covet your neighbor's house; you shall not covet your neighbor's wife. (ESV)

   Jeremiah 5:7–8 I supplied all their needs, yet they committed adultery and thronged to the houses of prostitutes. They are well-fed, lusty stallions, each neighing for another man's wife. (NIV)

   1 Thessalonians 4:6–7 Never harm or cheat a fellow believer in this matter by violating his wife, for the Lord avenges all such sins, as we have solemnly warned you before. God has called us to live holy lives, not impure lives. (NLT)

3. **Lustful thinking—imagining what it would be like to be with someone else—is mental and emotional adultery. It is sin. Like Job, men and women need to commit to moving their eyes and minds away from the object of lust.**

   Job 31:1 I made a covenant with my eyes not to look with lust at a young woman. (NLT)

   Matthew 5:28 But I say to you that everyone who looks at a woman with lustful intent has already committed adultery with her in his heart. (ESV)

Consequences of Adultery

1. **Adultery, like all sin, separates us from God. Only Jesus Christ offers us freedom.**

   1 Corinthians 6:9–13

2. **Adultery is destructive, one of the most harmful and hurtful events a couple can experience.**

   Proverbs 6:27–29, 32 Can a man carry fire next to his chest and his clothes not be burned? Or can one walk on hot coals and his feet not be scorched? So is he who goes in to his neighbor's wife;

none who touches her will go unpunished. . . . He who commits adultery lacks sense; he who does it destroys himself. (ESV)

Malachi 2:14 You cry out, "Why doesn't the Lord accept my worship?" I'll tell you why! Because the Lord witnessed the vows you and your wife made when you were young. But you have been unfaithful to her, though she remained your faithful partner, the wife of your marriage vows. (NLT)

Proverbs 5:20–23

Steps for Preventing Adultery

1. **Realize its source. Adultery happens when a person's heart is not focused on Christ.**

   Matthew 15:19 For out of the heart come evil thoughts, murders, adulteries, fornications, thefts, false witness, slanders. (NASB)

   Colossians 3:2 Set your mind on the things above, not on the things that are on earth. (NASB)

   Matthew 16:23; 2 Corinthians 5:17; Hebrews 12:1–2

2. **Adultery is prevented by changing our thinking and accepting it as the sin it is.**

   Romans 8:5–6 Those who are dominated by the sinful nature think about sinful things, but those who are controlled by the Holy Spirit think about things that please the Spirit. So letting your sinful nature control your mind leads to death. But letting the Spirit control your mind leads to life and peace. (NLT)

   Romans 12:1–2

3. **With God's help, temptation can be resisted.**

   1 Corinthians 10:13–14 No temptation has overtaken you but such as is common to man; and God is faithful, who will not allow you to be tempted beyond what you are able, but with the temptation will provide the way of escape also, so that you will be able to endure it. Therefore, my beloved, flee from idolatry [includes other sins]. (NASB)

4. **Our mind-set must be a renewed commitment to honor covenant vows.**

   Hebrews 13:4 Marriage is to be honored by all, and husbands and wives must be faithful to each other. God will judge those who are immoral and those who commit adultery. (GNT)
   Malachi 2:13–16

5. **Exercising self-control is a key factor. Be dependent on the Holy Spirit; accept his control.**

   1 Thessalonians 4:3–6 It is God's will that you should be sanctified: that you should avoid sexual immorality; that each of you should learn to control your own body in a way that is holy and honorable, not in passionate lust like the pagans, who do not know God; and that in this matter no one should wrong or take advantage of a brother or sister. (NIV)
   Galatians 5:16; Ephesians 4:30; 5:18; 1 Thessalonians 5:19

6. **We must accept God's wisdom through his Word.**

   Proverbs 2:16–18 Wisdom will save you also from the adulterous woman, from the wayward woman with her seductive words, who has left the partner of her youth and ignored the covenant she made before God. Surely her house leads down to death and her paths to the spirits of the dead. (NIV)
   Psalm 119:9, 11

7. **A healthy sexual relationship within marriage is helpful.**

   1 Corinthians 7:2–3 But because there is so much sexual immorality, each man should have his own wife, and each woman should have her own husband. The husband should fulfill his wife's sexual needs, and the wife should fulfill her husband's needs. (NLT) (See entire paragraph.)

If Adultery Has Occurred

1. **If you fall into this sin, confess, repent, and seek God's forgiveness and restoration with your spouse.**

   1 John 1:9 If we confess our sins, He is faithful and just to forgive us our sins and to cleanse us from all unrighteousness. (NKJV)

   Psalm 32:1, 5 Blessed is the one whose transgression is forgiven, whose sin is covered. . . . I acknowledged my sin to you, and I did not cover my iniquity; I said, "I will confess my transgressions to the Lord," and you forgave the iniquity of my sin. (ESV)

2. **If your spouse has failed in this area, and responds with confession and repentance, forgiveness and restoration are now your responsibility.**

   Colossians 3:12–13 Put on then, as God's chosen ones, holy and beloved, compassionate hearts, kindness, humility, meekness, and patience, bearing with one another and, if one has a complaint against another, forgiving each other; as the Lord has forgiven you, so you also must forgive. (ESV)

   Ephesians 4:32 Be kind to one another, tenderhearted, forgiving one another, as God in Christ forgave you. (ESV)

   Hosea 3:1 The Lord said to me, "Go again and show your love for a woman who is committing adultery with a lover. You must love her just as I still love the people of Israel, even though they turn to other gods and like to take offerings of raisins to idols." (GNT)

Practical Steps

- For help in preventing adultery, keep pictures of your spouse and children available for frequent viewing at home and at work. In your office, place them strategically to let others of the opposite sex know you are unavailable. Use them on business trips as well, to look at and show others.

- When tempting thoughts come, pray quickly for help. Pray, "Lord, please remove that thought from me," or "Lord, through your Spirit, I reject that thought."
- If adultery has happened, consider the possibility of how you might have contributed to the infidelity (your own or your spouse's). Take radical steps to prevent it from happening again (Matthew 5:29–30).
- Create a plan—how do you protect your faithfulness and avoid a compromising situation? Have safeguards in place—not being alone with and limiting your time with another man/woman.
- Seek restoration. Distance yourself from past relationships. Date your spouse. Pray daily for each other. Write letters to each other.

Resources

- *After Adultery* (booklet). Robert Jones. New Growth.
- *Help! My Spouse Has Been Unfaithful*. Mike Summers. Shepherd.
- *I Should Forgive, But . . . : Finding Release from the Bondage of Anger and Bitterness*. Chuck Lynch. Word.
- *Love Life for Every Married Couple: How to Fall in Love, Stay in Love, Rekindle Your Love*. Ed Wheat. Zondervan.
- *Loving Your Marriage Enough to Protect It*. Jerry Jenkins. Moody.
- "You Shall Not Commit Adultery" in *Pathway to Freedom: How God's Laws Guide Our Lives*. Alistair Begg. Moody.

Goals and Dreams

Starry-eyed? Super-excited? What possible superlatives can adequately describe a couple's excitement about being together as a married couple? Pundits might say "delusional," but who cares when you're on your honeymoon? Often the question is asked, "What are you looking forward to?" A part of our humanity as created in the image of God is anticipation, planning, and dreaming about good things for the future. What does God have in store for those who love him in return?

Priorities

See also **Career, Decision Making, Essential Disciplines, Finances, Materialism, Selfishness**

While the material below is numbered and has a logical progression, it is perhaps better to visualize God placed in a circle, at the very center of our existence, with various aspects of life surrounding and emitting forth from him. He must be at that center, especially with success and happiness in marriage at stake.

1. **We must first know God as the "root drive" and everything else as simply "file folders" beneath him. He is the great and sovereign Father God and Creator.**

   Isaiah 44:6 Thus says the LORD, the King of Israel and his Redeemer, the LORD of hosts: "I am the first and I am the last, and there is no God besides Me." (NASB)

   Isaiah 42:8 I am the LORD, that is My name; I will not give My glory to another, nor My praise to graven images. (NASB)

   Isaiah 43:10–13 "You are my witnesses," declares the LORD, "and my servant whom I have chosen, so that you may know and believe me and understand that I am he. Before me no god was formed, nor will there be one after me. I, even I, am the LORD, and apart from me there is no savior. I have revealed and saved and proclaimed—I, and not some foreign god among you. You are my witnesses," declares the LORD, "that I am God. Yes, and from ancient days I am he. No one can deliver out of my hand. When I act, who can reverse it?" (NIV)

2. **Our lives are therefore lived before an audience of One. Our purpose for living must be to bring glory to God as we serve him. All dreams and goals must reflect this.**

Psalm 115:1 Not to us, O Lord, not to us, but to your name give glory, for the sake of your steadfast love and your faithfulness! (ESV)

1 Chronicles 16:24–25, 28–29 Declare his glory among the nations, his marvelous works among all the peoples! For great is the Lord, and greatly to be praised, and he is to be held in awe above all gods. . . . Ascribe to the Lord, O families of the peoples, ascribe to the Lord glory and strength! Ascribe to the Lord the glory due his name. (ESV)

Isaiah 43:7 Bring all who claim me as their God, for I have made them for my glory. It was I who created them. (NLT)

Haggai 1:8 Go up to the hills and bring wood and build the house, that I may take pleasure in it and that I may be glorified, says the Lord. (ESV) (See context of priorities.)

1 Corinthians 10:31 So, whether you eat or drink, or whatever you do, do all to the glory of God. (ESV)

Ephesians 5:7–8; 6:5–7; Colossians 3:23; 2 Corinthians 5:9; Hebrews 13:15–16, 20–21

3. **Our Creator expects us to give him the first and most important place in our lives.**

Matthew 22:35–38 And one of them, a lawyer, asked him [Jesus] a question to test him. "Teacher, which is the great commandment in the Law?" And he said to him, "You shall love the Lord your God with all your heart and with all your soul and with all your mind. This is the great and first commandment." (ESV)

Matthew 6:31–33 Therefore do not be anxious, saying, "What shall we eat?" or "What shall we drink?" or "What shall we wear?" For the Gentiles seek after all these things, and your heavenly Father knows that you need them all. But seek first the kingdom of God and his righteousness, and all these things will be added to you. (ESV)

Deuteronomy 10:20–21

4. **Family—husband/wife and children—must be a priority.**

   Ephesians 5:25–31 Husbands, love your wives, as Christ loved the church and gave himself up for her, that he might sanctify her, having cleansed her by the washing of water with the word, so that he might present the church to himself in splendor, without spot or wrinkle or any such thing, that she might be holy and without blemish. In the same way husbands should love their wives as their own bodies. He who loves his wife loves himself. For no one ever hated his own flesh, but nourishes and cherishes it, just as Christ does the church, because we are members of his body. Therefore a man shall leave his father and mother and hold fast to his wife, and the two shall become one flesh. (ESV)

   Ephesians 6:4 Fathers, do not provoke your children to anger, but bring them up in the discipline and instruction of the Lord. (ESV)

   Deuteronomy 6:6–7; Psalm 127; 1 Thessalonians 2:10–12

5. **Placing others ahead of ourselves must be high on our list of priorities. Loving and serving!**

   Matthew 22:39–40 And a second [after the first commandment—loving God] is like it: You shall love your neighbor as yourself. On these two commandments depend all the Law and the Prophets. (ESV)

   Galatians 5:13–14 For you were called to freedom, brothers. Only do not use your freedom as an opportunity for the flesh, but through love serve one another. For the whole law is fulfilled in one word: "You shall love your neighbor as yourself." (ESV)

   Philippians 2:3–4 Do nothing from selfish ambition or conceit, but in humility count others more significant than yourselves. Let each of you look not only to his own interests, but also to the interests of others. (ESV)

Practical Steps

- Both marriage partners should be willing to think sacrificially in regard to their spouse and his/her desires, dreams, goals, and material possessions.

- Evaluate carefully where your priorities lie. What is really first? What do you think about the most? Is selfishness a problem? Ask God to convict you and change your heart.
- Are you a workaholic? Commit to leaving work behind when you come home to your family. Be realistic in the hours you spend at work.
- Realize that heavy involvement in church does not necessarily mean that God is first in your life. There are other priorities that God wants us to establish. Too much time spent in church could mean you are neglecting your family.

Resources

- *Balancing Life's Demands: Biblical Priorities for a Busy Life* (DVD series). Chip Ingram. Living on the Edge Ministries.
- *Balancing the Christian Life*. Charles Ryrie. Moody.
- *Priorities: Mastering Time Management* (booklet). James Petty. P&R.
- *The Pursuit of God*. A. W. Tozer. Christian Publications.

Career

See also **Finances, Job Loss, Materialism, Priorities**

Everyone needs money to live. Working diligently for financial needs and obligations is both logical and scriptural. A strong work ethic is essential for the strength of the marriage. One question for couples is "How much money is really necessary?" A related question involves the amount of time consumed working. Is the family relationship hurting because of lack of time spent at home by one or both partners? Are you committed to biblical relationships either as an employee or employer?

1. **A man who chooses to be a husband and father must make that calling his first and foremost career responsibility. Family before work! Balance is crucial.**

   Ephesians 5:25, 28–29 Husbands, love your wives, as Christ loved the church and gave himself up for her. . . . In the same way husbands should love their wives as their own bodies. He who loves his wife loves himself. For no one ever hated his own flesh, but nourishes and cherishes it, just as Christ does the church. (ESV)

   Deuteronomy 6:6–7 And these words that I command you today shall be on your heart. You shall teach them diligently to your children, and shall talk of them when you sit in your house, and when you walk by the way, and when you lie down, and when you rise. (ESV)

   Psalm 128:1–4; Matthew 7:9–11

2. **For a woman who chooses to be a wife and mother, whether she works outside the home or not, her first and foremost**

responsibility needs to be caring for her home and her children. Family before work! Balance is crucial.

Proverbs 14:1 The wise woman builds her house, but the foolish tears it down with her own hands. (NASB)

Titus 2:3–5 Older women likewise are to be reverent in their behavior, not malicious gossips nor enslaved to much wine, teaching what is good, so that they may encourage the young women to love their husbands, to love their children, to be sensible, pure, workers at home, kind, being subject to their own husbands, so that the word of God will not be dishonored. (NASB)

1 Timothy 5:14 So I would have younger widows marry, bear children, manage their households, and give the adversary no occasion for slander. (ESV)

3. **Seeking God's wisdom in our career/employment choices is vital.**

James 1:5 But if any of you lacks wisdom, let him ask of God, who gives to all generously and without reproach, and it will be given to him. (NASB)

Psalm 111:10 The way to become wise is to honor the Lord; he gives sound judgment to all who obey his commands. (GNT)

Proverbs 4:5; 14:33; James 3:17

4. **As we place total trust in God, allowing him to give us direction for the pathways of our lives, we can be certain that he will lead us.**

Jeremiah 6:16 This is what the Lord says: "Stand at the crossroads and look; ask for the ancient paths, ask where the good way is, and walk in it, and you will find rest for your souls." (NIV)

Psalm 20:4–5 May he grant your heart's desires and make all your plans succeed. May we shout for joy when we hear of your victory and raise a victory banner in the name of our God. May the Lord answer all your prayers. (NLT)

Proverbs 3:5–6

5. **All work must be done ultimately for God's glory and with his reputation in mind.**

Ecclesiastes 12:13–14 The end of the matter; all has been heard. Fear God and keep his commandments, for this is the whole duty of man. For God will bring every deed into judgment, with every secret thing, whether good or evil. (ESV)

Psalm 115:1 Not to us, O Lord, not to us, but to your name give glory, for the sake of your steadfast love and your faithfulness! (ESV)

Colossians 3:23 Whatever you do, do your work heartily, as for the Lord rather than for men. (NASB)

1 Corinthians 10:31; Colossians 3:17; 1 Peter 4:11

6. **Respectful obedience is due our employer. If you are the employer, justice and fairness are due to employees. (To apply the following verses to today's culture, substitute "workers" for "slaves" and "employers" for "masters.")**

Ephesians 6:5–8 Slaves, obey your earthly masters with respect and fear, and with sincerity of heart, just as you would obey Christ. Obey them not only to win their favor when their eye is on you, but as slaves of Christ, doing the will of God from your heart. Serve wholeheartedly, as if you were serving the Lord, not people, because you know that the Lord will reward each one for whatever good they do, whether they are slave or free. (NIV)

Ephesians 6:9 Masters, treat your slaves in the same way. Do not threaten them, since you know that he who is both their Master and yours is in heaven, and there is no favoritism with him. (NIV)

Colossians 3:22–24; 4:1; Titus 2:9–10; 1 Timothy 6:1–2; 1 Peter 2:18–19

7. **Our testimony in the workplace must be exemplary. Integrity, honesty, and responsibility must be in place.**

Proverbs 3:3–4 Never let loyalty and kindness leave you! Tie them around your neck as a reminder. Write them deep within your heart. Then you will find favor with both God and people, and you will earn a good reputation. (NLT)

2 Corinthians 8:21; 1 Timothy 3:7

Practical Steps

- If you are one who moves quickly from job to job, ask others who have longevity in their fields how they are able to stay so long. Move toward responsibility, discipline, and patience in your workplace.
- A couple should consider the possibility of living on one income (i.e., buying less), with one spouse staying home to care for the home.
- As a parent, write a list of pros and cons for employment. Are there ways to change your lifestyle as a couple to be home with your children?
- If you are employed outside your home, evaluate what your job takes out of you physically, emotionally, mentally, and spiritually. Does your home suffer? Do changes need to be made? Also, is it really worth it financially as you count the increased cost of travel, clothes, or child care? Does your income actually increase that much?
- Study Joshua 1:8—"Study this Book of Instruction continually. Meditate on it day and night so you will be sure to obey everything written in it. Only then you will prosper and succeed in all you do." (NLT). What is God's way for successful living?

Resources

- *The Call: Finding and Fulfilling the Central Purpose of Your Life*. Os Guinness. Thomas Nelson.
- *Choosing Your Career: The Christian's Decision Manual*. Martin Clark. P&R.
- *Life in the Spirit: Marriage, Home, and Work*. Martyn Lloyd-Jones. Baker.
- *Real Prosperity*. Gene Getz. Moody.
- *Work Matters*. Tom Nelson. Crossway.

Decision Making

See also **Contentment, Finances, Materialism, Priorities**

Two individuals are now united as one. Decision making has changed; decisions should reflect the oneness of marriage. What is best for your day-to-day relationship together? What is best for your anticipated future—children, career, dreams, and goals? What is the wise decision that will bring glory to God?

1. **Each spouse must be willing to take into account the other's viewpoint and desires. How do we live and function with the very best in mind for our marriage?**

   Philippians 2:3–5 Do nothing out of selfish ambition or vain conceit. Rather, in humility value others above yourselves, not looking to your own interests but each of you to the interests of the others. In your relationships with one another, have the same mindset as Christ Jesus. (NIV) (See context for Christ's attitude.)

2. **Ask—what is the wise thing to do? Seek wisdom in light of choices made in the past, in light of your present situation, and thinking of your future together, your dreams and goals.**

   James 1:5 But if any of you lack wisdom, you should pray to God, who will give it to you; because God gives generously and graciously to all. (GNT)

   James 3:17 But the wisdom from above is pure first of all; it is also peaceful, gentle, and friendly; it is full of compassion and produces a harvest of good deeds; it is free from prejudice and hypocrisy. (GNT)

   Psalm 25:4–5 Teach me your ways, O Lord; make them known to me. Teach me to live according to your truth, for you are my God, who saves me. I always trust in you. (GNT)

3. **Prayer is essential; God's leading is desired in the making of good choices.**

   Matthew 7:7–8 Ask, and it will be given to you; seek, and you will find; knock, and it will be opened to you. For everyone who asks receives, and he who seeks finds, and to him who knocks it will be opened. (NKJV)

   Proverbs 16:9 The mind of man plans his way, but the LORD directs his steps. (NASB)

   Colossians 1:9–10 For this reason we also, since the day we heard it, do not cease to pray for you, and to ask that you may be filled with the knowledge of His will in all wisdom and spiritual understanding; that you may walk worthy of the Lord, fully pleasing Him, being fruitful in every good work and increasing in the knowledge of God. (NKJV)

   Proverbs 3:5–6; Jeremiah 10:23–24

4. **Always consider wise advice/counsel from others.**

   Proverbs 11:14 Where there is no guidance, a people falls, but in an abundance of counselors there is safety. (ESV)

   Proverbs 15:22 Without counsel plans fail, but with many advisers they succeed. (ESV)

   Proverbs 14:15 The simple believes everything, but the prudent gives thought to his steps. (ESV)

5. **Our motivation in decision-making must be obedience to God and a desire to please him. Expressing thanksgiving for his leading should follow.**

   Deuteronomy 10:12–13 And now, Israel, what does the LORD your God require of you? He requires only that you fear the LORD your God, and live in a way that pleases him, and love him and serve him with all your heart and soul. And you must always obey the LORD's commands and decrees that I am giving you today for your own good. (NLT)

   Psalm 40:8 I desire to do your will, my God; your law is within my heart. (NIV)

   Jeremiah 6:16 This is what the LORD says: "Stop at the crossroads and look around. Ask for the old, godly way, and walk in it. Travel its path, and you will find rest for your souls." (NLT)

Ephesians 5:8–11 For once you were full of darkness, but now you have light from the Lord. So live as people of light! For this light within you produces only what is good and right and true. Carefully determine what pleases the Lord. (NLT)

1 Thessalonians 5:16–18 Rejoice always; pray without ceasing; in everything give thanks; for this is God's will for you in Christ Jesus. (NASB)

Psalm 104:34; 2 Corinthians 5:9–10; 1 Thessalonians 2:4; Hebrews 13:2; James 4:13–15

Practical Steps

- Study Joshua's decision to serve the Lord: Joshua 24:14–15.
- Involve other godly, mature couples who will counsel and pray with you.
- Commit to doing God's will no matter where it may lead.
- Write out pros and cons for decisions you must make. Study Scripture to know God's thinking on the issues.
- Spend time in fasting, prayer, and meditation. Ask for wisdom and discernment.
- Consider the many "wait on God" teachings of Scripture. Commit to taking enough time for making a wise decision.

Resources

- *Designing a Lifestyle that Pleases God*. Patricia Ennis and Lisa C. Tatlock. Moody.
- *Finding God When You Need Him Most*. Chip Ingram. Baker.
- *God's Guidance: A Slow and Certain Light*. Elisabeth Elliot. Revell.
- *God's Will: Guidance for Everyday Decisions*. J. I. Packer. Baker.
- *Step by Step: Divine Guidance for Ordinary Christians.* James C. Petty. P&R.

Finances

See also **Decision Making, Materialism, Priorities**

What you do with your money is the number one point of contention for many couples. Talk about a "red flag" issue—this is it. She comes from a large family where spending on other than the essentials was difficult. His background is a family with one sibling, who though not wealthy was provided with lots of extras. How does being a follower of Christ make a difference in our attitudes about money?

1. **Everything we have comes from God and belongs ultimately to him.**

   1 Chronicles 29:11–12 Yours, O Lord, is the greatness and the power and the glory and the victory and the majesty, for all that is in the heavens and in the earth is yours. Yours is the kingdom, O Lord, and you are exalted as head above all. Both riches and honor come from you, and you rule over all. In your hand are power and might, and in your hand it is to make great and to give strength to all. (ESV)

   Deuteronomy 8:18 And you shall remember the Lord your God, for it is He who gives you power to get wealth, that He may establish His covenant which He swore to your fathers, as it is this day. (NKJV)

   Psalm 50:12 If I were hungry, I would not tell you, for all the world is mine and everything in it. (NLT)

2. **Jesus had more to say about money than almost any other subject.**

   Matthew 6:19–24 Do not lay up for yourselves treasures on earth, where moth and rust destroy and where thieves break in and steal, but lay up for yourselves treasures in heaven, where neither moth nor rust destroys and where thieves do not break in and steal. For where your treasure is, there your heart will be also. The eye is the lamp of the body. So, if your eye is healthy, your whole body will be full of light, but if your eye is bad, your whole body will be full of darkness. If then the light in you is darkness, how great is the darkness! No one can serve two masters, for either he will hate the one and love the other, or he will be devoted to the one and despise the other. You cannot serve God and money. (ESV)

Matthew 6:31–34 Therefore do not be anxious, saying, "What shall we eat?" or "What shall we drink?" or "What shall we wear?" For the Gentiles seek after all these things, and your heavenly Father knows that you need them all. But seek first the kingdom of God and his righteousness, and all these things will be added to you. Therefore do not be anxious about tomorrow, for tomorrow will be anxious for itself. Sufficient for the day is its own trouble. (ESV)

Luke 12:15; Ecclesiastes 5:10

3. **Paul's commands to Timothy are priceless for handling our finances.**

1 Timothy 6:6–11 But godliness with contentment is great gain, for we brought nothing into the world, and we cannot take anything out of the world. But if we have food and clothing, with these we will be content. But those who desire to be rich fall into temptation, into a snare, into many senseless and harmful desires that plunge people into ruin and destruction. For the love of money is a root of all kinds of evils. It is through this craving that some have wandered away from the faith and pierced themselves with many pangs. But as for you, O man of God, flee these things. Pursue righteousness, godliness, faith, love, steadfastness, gentleness. (ESV)

4. **Enjoying what God has given us is a part of his plan.**

Ecclesiastes 5:18–20 Behold, what I have seen to be good and fitting is to eat and drink and find enjoyment in all the toil with which one toils under the sun the few days of his life that God has given him, for this is his lot. Everyone also to whom God has given wealth and possessions and power to enjoy them, and to accept his lot and rejoice in his toil—this is the gift of God. For he will not much remember the days of his life because God keeps him occupied with joy in his heart. (ESV)

1 Timothy 6:17–19 As for the rich in this present age, charge them not to be haughty, nor to set their hopes on the uncertainty of riches, but on God, who richly provides us with everything to enjoy. They are to do good, to be rich in good works, to be generous and ready to share, thus storing up treasure for themselves as a good foundation for the future, so that they may take hold of that which is truly life. (ESV)

5. **Sharing with others who are needy and giving back to God should be a part of our financial planning. Grace giving can include the tithing standard of the Old Testament. The Old Testament laws help us understand God's mind and heart about giving. See "Spiritual Disciplines."**

Proverbs 3:9–10 Honor the Lord with your wealth and with the best part of everything you produce. Then he will fill your barns with grain, and your vats will overflow with good wine. (NLT)

2 Corinthians 9:6–7 Remember this—a farmer who plants only a few seeds will get a small crop. But the one who plants generously will get a generous crop. You must each decide in your heart how much to give. And don't give reluctantly or in response to pressure. For God loves a person who gives cheerfully. (NLT)

Leviticus 27:30–33; Malachi 3:8; Romans 6:14–15

6. **Study these admonitions from Proverbs—10:15; 11:4; 18:11; 23:5; 28:20. For variety, try the New Living Translation.**

Practical Steps

- Having an emergency savings account is a wise plan. At least two months' expenses saved in reserve will alleviate times of stress.

- Set up an investment plan for your future years as life slows down. Save consistently.
- Seriously consider the benefits of living on just one income.
- Maintain a budget plan with financial goals. Need help budgeting? Crown Financial Ministries is an excellent site (www.crown.org).
- If credit card use is out of control, stop using, pay them down, and cut them up.
- Sign up for a Financial Peace University (Dave Ramsey) course.

Resources

- *Counterfeit Gods: The Empty Promises of Money, Sex, and Power*. Timothy Keller. Dutton.
- "Financial Dealings" in *Character Counts*. Rod Handley. Cross Training.
- *Money, Possessions, and Eternity*. Randy Alcorn. Tyndale.
- *Real Prosperity*. Gene Getz. Moody.
- *Sex and Money: Pleasures That Leave You Empty and Grace That Satisfies*. Paul Tripp. Crossway.
- *The Total Money Makeover* (highly recommended, audio book available). Dave Ramsey. Thomas Nelson.

Materialism

See also **Contentment, Decision Making, Finances**

Constant communication is crucial as a couple considers what is really needed as opposed to what they would like to have. Each needs to be knowledgeable of the other's spending habits while they were growing up, patterns of purchases when each was still single, and the realities of current income as a married couple. God's Word has much to teach about possessions and heart attitude.

1. **Wealth in this life doesn't even begin to compare with treasures in heaven.**

   Matthew 6:19–21 Do not store up for yourselves treasures on earth, where moth and rust destroy, and where thieves break in and steal. But store up for yourselves treasures in heaven, where neither moth nor rust destroys, and where thieves do not break in or steal; for where your treasure is, there your heart will be also. (NASB)

   1 Corinthians 3:11–15 For no man can lay a foundation other than the one which is laid, which is Jesus Christ. Now if any man builds on the foundation with gold, silver, precious stones, wood, hay, straw, each man's work will become evident; for the day will show it because it is to be revealed with fire, and the fire itself will test the quality of each man's work. If any man's work which he has built on it remains, he will receive a reward. If any man's work is burned up, he will suffer loss; but he himself will be saved, yet so as through fire. (NASB)

2. **A trap of destruction awaits those who have an excessive passion for more possessions. There will never be enough.**

   Psalm 73:2–3, 7 But as for me, I almost lost my footing. My feet were slipping, and I was almost gone. For I envied the proud when I saw them prosper despite their wickedness. . . . These fat cats have everything their hearts could ever wish for! (NLT)

   1 Timothy 6:6–9 Yet true godliness with contentment is itself great wealth. After all, we brought nothing with us when we came into the world, and we can't take anything with us when we leave it. So if we have enough food and clothing, let us be content. But people who long to be rich fall into temptation and are trapped by many foolish and harmful desires that plunge them into ruin and destruction. (NLT)

   James 5:1–3, 5 Look here, you rich people: Weep and groan with anguish because of all the terrible troubles ahead of you. Your wealth is rotting away, and your fine clothes are moth-eaten rags. Your gold and silver are corroded. The very wealth you were counting on will eat away your flesh like fire. This corroded treasure you have hoarded will testify against you on the day of judgment. . . . You have spent your years on earth in luxury, satisfying your every desire. You have fattened yourselves for the day of slaughter. (NLT)

   Proverbs 28:25 Greed causes fighting; trusting the LORD leads to prosperity. (NLT)

   Proverbs 23:4–5 Don't wear yourself out trying to get rich. Be wise enough to know when to quit. In the blink of an eye wealth disappears, for it will sprout wings and fly away like an eagle. (NLT)

3. **Godly men and women must prioritize. Which has become more important—wealth or our walk with God? What is the wise choice?**

   Proverbs 30:8–9 Keep deception and lies far from me, give me neither poverty nor riches; feed me with the food that is my portion, that I not be full and deny You and say, "Who is the LORD?" Or that I not be in want and steal, and profane the name of my God. (NASB)

1 Timothy 6:10 For the love of money is a root of all kinds of evil, for which some have strayed from the faith in their greediness, and pierced themselves through with many sorrows. (NKJV)

1 John 2:15 Do not love the world or the things in the world. If anyone loves the world, the love of the Father is not in him. (NKJV)

4. **Material possessions will never provide the security we desire.**

Jeremiah 9:23–24 Thus says the Lord: "Let not the wise man glory in his wisdom, let not the mighty man glory in his might, nor let the rich man glory in his riches; but let him who glories glory in this, that he understands and knows Me, that I am the Lord, exercising lovingkindness, judgment, and righteousness in the earth. For in these I delight," says the Lord. (NKJV)

Isaiah 58:11 The Lord will guide you continually, and satisfy your soul in drought, and strengthen your bones; you shall be like a watered garden, and like a spring of water, whose waters do not fail. (NKJV)

Luke 12:15 And he said to them, "Take care, and be on your guard against all covetousness, for one's life does not consist in the abundance of his possessions." (ESV)

1 Timothy 6:17 As for the rich in this present age, charge them not to be haughty, nor to set their hopes on the uncertainty of riches, but on God, who richly provides us with everything to enjoy. (ESV)

Psalm 39:4–6; Proverbs 28:6; Hebrews 13:5

5. **Giving willingly to God through church, ministries, and assisting those less fortunate is a blessing to the giver and the recipient.**

2 Corinthians 9:6–8 Remember this: Whoever sows sparingly will also reap sparingly, and whoever sows generously will also reap generously. Each of you should give what you have decided in your heart to give, not reluctantly or under compulsion, for God loves a cheerful giver. And God is able to bless you abundantly, so that in all things at all times, having all that you need, you will abound in every good work. (NIV)

1 Timothy 6:18–19 They are to do good, to be rich in good works, to be generous and ready to share, thus storing up treasure for themselves as a good foundation for the future, so that they may take hold of that which is truly life. (ESV)

Proverbs 31:8–9 Speak up for those who cannot speak for themselves, for the rights of all who are destitute. Speak up and judge fairly; defend the rights of the poor and needy. (NIV)

6. **The Bible gives us some principles for avoiding materialism.**

1 Timothy 6:11 But you, O man of God, flee these things [love of money] and pursue righteousness, godliness, faith, love, patience, gentleness. (NKJV)

Philippians 4:11–13 And I am not saying this because I feel neglected, for I have learned to be satisfied with what I have. I know what it is to be in need and what it is to have more than enough. I have learned this secret, so that anywhere, at any time, I am content, whether I am full or hungry, whether I have too much or too little. I have the strength to face all conditions by the power that Christ gives me. (GNT)

Colossians 3:1–5 You have been raised to life with Christ, so set your hearts on the things that are in heaven, where Christ sits on his throne at the right side of God. Keep your minds fixed on things there, not on things here on earth. For you have died, and your life is hidden with Christ in God. Your real life is Christ and when he appears, then you too will appear with him and share his glory! (GNT)

7. **Never forget that the source of everything we have is God. It all belongs to him.**

Deuteronomy 8:11–14 Take care lest you forget the LORD your God by not keeping his commandments and his rules and his statutes, which I command you today, lest, when you have eaten and are full and have built good houses and live in them, and when your herds and flocks multiply and your silver and gold is multiplied and all that you have is multiplied, then your heart be lifted up, and you forget the LORD your God, who brought you out of the land of Egypt, out of the house of slavery. (ESV)

Practical Steps

- Evaluate purchases, prayerfully taking time to consider. For major purchases, never buy the first time you look. Have a cooling-off period. Evaluate real needs versus wants.
- Avoid purchasing a new car. Find something a couple of years old with low miles. This will save a lot of money.
- Ask for wisdom for electronic updates. Do you really need all those extra features you probably won't use anyway?
- Follow a budget—have a plan and goal—and set limits. Make giving to God the first check you write each pay period.
- If "things" are your gods, repent, confess, and pray for renewal. Commit to lifestyle change. Seek accountability from a wiser, more mature couple.
- Work at living on one income if this would benefit your family life.

Resources

- *Counterfeit Gods: The Empty Promises of Money, Sex, and Power*. Timothy Keller. Dutton.
- *George Müller: Children's Champion*. Irene Howat. Christian Focus. (This is a biography of a man who trusted God totally for material needs.)
- *Money, Possessions, and Eternity*. Randy Alcorn. Tyndale.
- *Real Prosperity: Biblical Principles of Material Possessions*. Gene Getz. Moody.
- *When Money Runs Out* (booklet). James Petty. New Growth.

Emotional Needs

Emotions are feelings, often subjective, that occur as we respond to events or stimuli in our lives. Something happens that affects how we feel, positively or negatively. The more negative the event, the stronger the arousal or agitation can be. How we express those feelings can greatly affect the quality and success of our marriage. This section is about handling those negative emotions in a godly, biblical manner.

Anger

See also **Disappointment, Forgiving Each Other, Selfishness**

Biblical teaching about anger includes that which is righteous and that which is sinful. Few would deny that sinful anger is a destructive emotion. Anger in marriage, inappropriately expressed and unresolved over any period of time, becomes lethal to the longevity and happiness of that relationship. It must be brought under control, dealt with, resolved, and removed.

Righteous/Justified Anger—Appropriate when Someone Has Sinned

1. **God himself expresses righteous anger against sin.**

   Exodus 32:9–10 Then the LORD said, "I have seen how stubborn and rebellious these people are. Now leave me alone so my fierce anger can blaze against them, and I will destroy them. Then I will make you, Moses, into a great nation." (NLT)
   Deuteronomy 9:8

2. **Jesus expressed righteous anger.**

   Mark 3:5 He looked around at them angrily and was deeply saddened by their hard hearts. (NLT)
   Mark 11:15; Matthew 21:12–13 (in the temple)

3. **The believer can also express righteous anger.**

   Ephesians 4:26 BE ANGRY, AND yet DO NOT SIN; do not let the sun go down on your anger. (NASB)

Unrighteous/Sinful Anger—When We Choose an Angry Response because of Personally Being Affronted in Some Way

1. **Anger is included in a list of disturbing sins.**

   Galatians 5:19–21 What human nature does is quite plain. It shows itself in immoral, filthy, and indecent actions; in worship of idols and witchcraft. People become enemies and they fight; they become jealous, angry, and ambitious. They separate into parties and groups; they are envious, get drunk, have orgies, and do other things like these. I warn you now as I have before: those who do these things will not possess the Kingdom of God. (GNT)

   Proverbs 29:22 An angry man stirs up strife, and a furious man abounds in transgression. (NKJV)

2. **Anger is a loss of self-control and must be removed and replaced with kindness and forgiveness.**

   Proverbs 29:11 A fool always loses his temper, but a wise man holds it back. (NASB)

   Ephesians 4:31–32 Let all bitterness and wrath and anger and clamor and slander be put away from you, along with all malice. Be kind to one another, tenderhearted, forgiving one another, as God in Christ forgave you. (ESV)

   Psalm 37:8; Colossians 3:8

3. **To avoid anger, husbands and wives need to listen more, talk less, and respond slowly. Each must sincerely work to understand the other.**

   James 1:19–20 Remember this, my dear friends! Everyone must be quick to listen, but slow to speak and slow to become angry. Human anger does not achieve God's righteous purpose. (GNT)

   Proverbs 14:17 People with a hot temper do foolish things; wiser people remain calm. (GNT)

   Proverbs 20:3 It is to one's honor to avoid strife, but every fool is quick to quarrel. (NIV)

   Ecclesiastes 7:9

4. **Married couples must be doubly cautious in ridding themselves of anger. Inappropriate or poorly expressed anger is a major factor in family problems and a poor example to children.**

   Ephesians 5:25, 28–29 Husbands, love your wives, just as Christ loved the church and gave himself up for her. . . . In this same way, husbands ought to love their wives as their own bodies. He who loves his wife loves himself. After all, no one ever hated their own body, but they feed and care for their body, just as Christ does the church. (NIV)

   Colossians 3:19 Husbands, love your wives and do not be harsh with them. (NIV)

   Colossians 3:21 Fathers, do not embitter your children, or they will become discouraged. (NIV)

   Ephesians 6:4 Fathers, do not exasperate your children. (NIV)

Responding to Anger

1. **Practicing a gentle and kind response and avoiding an angry response can effectively reduce episodes of anger.**

   Proverbs 15:1 A gentle answer turns away wrath, but a harsh word stirs up anger. (NASB)

2. **Do not respond to anger with anger. Breathe grace and handle anger with a godly reply.**

   Romans 12:19 Beloved, never avenge yourselves, but leave it to the wrath of God, for it is written, "Vengeance is mine, I will repay, says the Lord." (ESV)

   Proverbs 20:22 Don't say, "I will get even for this wrong." Wait for the Lord to handle the matter. (NLT)

3. **For any anger issue between you and your spouse, work on taking care of it as soon as possible. Develop/implement a conscious plan for resolution.**

   Ephesians 4:26–27 And don't sin by letting anger control you. Don't let the sun go down while you are still angry, for anger gives a foothold to the devil. (NLT)

   Psalm 4:4 Be angry, and do not sin; ponder in your own hearts on your beds, and be silent. (ESV)

4. **Practice patience—the opposite of anger.**

   Proverbs 14:29 Whoever is patient has great understanding, but one who is quick-tempered displays folly. (NIV)

   Proverbs 15:18 A hot-tempered person stirs up conflict, but the one who is patient calms a quarrel. (NIV)

   Proverbs 16:32 Better a patient person than a warrior, one with self-control than one who takes a city. (NIV)

Practical Steps

- Think about past times when your spouse was angry. Review the causes and/or words that you used that helped trigger the anger. Take steps to avoid those sparks.
- Do not attempt to reason with your spouse when they are angry—wait until you both can communicate more calmly, with reason, not emotion.
- Every time you confess your anger to God (and others you have affected), redirect your energy toward a solution to the problem.
- Try this strategy: each person writes a list of his/her own problems to be worked on, and then compare your lists. This would aid in avoiding outbursts.

Resources

- *Anger: Escaping the Maze* (booklet). David Powlison. P&R.
- *Living with an Angry Spouse* (booklet). Ed Welch. New Growth.

- *Overcoming Emotions That Destroy: Practical Help for Those Angry Feelings That Ruin Relationships.* Chip Ingram. Baker.
- "Sinful Anger" in *Feelings and Faith: Cultivating Godly Emotions in the Christian Life.* Brian Borgman. Crossway.
- *Uprooting Anger* (booklet). Robert Jones. P&R.

Anxiety

See also **Abuse, Disappointment, Finances, Grief, Health, Job Loss, Trials**

Anxiety is a human response to the unknown. Fear is the anticipation of what could go wrong, or what might or might not happen. Not knowing what the future will bring leads to apprehension about life's uncertainties. Being married creates a whole new set of unknowns. Often, the main issue is trusting God no matter what comes.

Selected Key Anxiety Issues for Couples

1. **If anxiety is about the basic essentials for life, Jesus has that covered.**

   Matthew 6:31–34 So do not worry, saying, "What shall we eat?" or "What shall we drink?" or "What shall we wear?" For the pagans run after all these things, and your heavenly Father knows that you need them. But seek first his kingdom and his righteousness, and all these things will be given to you as well. Therefore do not worry about tomorrow, for tomorrow will worry about itself. Each day has enough trouble of its own. (NIV)

2. **No matter what our status in life, contentment in God's provision is possible.**

   Philippians 4:12–13, 19 I know what it is to be in need, and I know what it is to have plenty. I have learned the secret of being content in any and every situation, whether well fed or hungry, whether living in plenty or in want. I can do all this through him who gives me strength. . . . And my God will meet all your needs according to the riches of his glory in Christ Jesus. (NIV)

3. **Note these instructions concerning the choices and direction your life together should take.**

 Proverbs 3:1–2 My son, do not forget my teaching, but keep my commands in your heart, for they will prolong your life many years and bring you peace and prosperity. (NIV)

 Proverbs 3:5–6 Trust in the Lord with all your heart and lean not on your own understanding; in all your ways submit to him, and he will make your paths straight. (NIV)

 Proverbs 11:14 Where there is no guidance, a people falls, but in an abundance of counselors there is safety. (ESV)

4. **Do not have concern for investment plans—spending, saving, giving.**

 James 4:13–15 Come now, you who say, "Today or tomorrow we will go into such and such a town and spend a year there and trade and make a profit"—yet you do not know what tomorrow will bring. What is your life? For you are a mist that appears for a little time and then vanishes. Instead you ought to say, "If the Lord wills, we will live and do this or that." (ESV)

5. **If you worry over past sins, handle them biblically with repentance and forgiveness.**

 Psalm 103:10–12 He does not deal with us according to our sins, nor repay us according to our iniquities. For as high as the heavens are above the earth, so great is his steadfast love toward those who fear him; as far as the east is from the west, so far does he remove our transgressions from us. (ESV)

 Micah 7:18–19 Who is a God like you, pardoning iniquity and passing over transgression for the remnant of his inheritance? He does not retain his anger forever, because he delights in steadfast love. He will again have compassion on us; he will tread our iniquities underfoot. You will cast all our sins into the depths of the sea. (ESV)

6. **For concern over resisting temptation, know that God has a plan for relief.**

    1 Corinthians 10:13 No temptation has overtaken you that is not common to man. God is faithful, and he will not let you be tempted beyond your ability, but with the temptation he will also provide the way of escape, that you may be able to endure it. (ESV)

7. **If you are struggling with health issues, trust that God's grace can help us walk the path of uncertainty and adjustment.**

    2 Corinthians 12:7–10 There was given me a thorn in the flesh, a messenger of Satan to torment me—to keep me from exalting myself! Concerning this I implored the Lord three times that it might leave me. And He has said to me, "My grace is sufficient for you, for power is perfected in weakness." Most gladly, therefore, I will rather boast about my weaknesses, so that the power of Christ may dwell in me. Therefore I am well content with weaknesses, with insults, with distresses, with persecutions, with difficulties, for Christ's sake; for when I am weak, then I am strong. (NASB)

    Jude 24–25 Now to Him who is able to keep you from stumbling, and to make you stand in the presence of His glory blameless with great joy, to the only God our Savior, through Jesus Christ our Lord, be glory, majesty, dominion and authority, before all time and now and forever. (NASB)

8. **The world seems so out of control. Is God really in charge?**

    Psalm 93:1–2 The Lord reigns, he is robed in majesty; the Lord is robed in majesty and armed with strength; indeed, the world is established, firm and secure. Your throne was established long ago; you are from all eternity. (NIV)

    Daniel 7:13–14 In my vision at night I looked, and there before me was one like a son of man [Christ], coming with the clouds of heaven. He approached the Ancient of Days [God, the Father] and was led into his presence. He was given authority, glory and sovereign power; all nations and peoples of every language worshiped him. His dominion is an everlasting dominion that will not pass away, and his kingdom is one that will never be destroyed. (NIV)

Philippians 2:9–11 Therefore God exalted him to the highest place and gave him the name that is above every name, that at the name of Jesus every knee should bow, in heaven and on earth and under the earth, and every tongue acknowledge that Jesus Christ is Lord, to the glory of God the Father. (NIV)

Psalm 2

Practical Steps

- Study and meditate on Philippians 4:6–7. List specific ways you can practice this when anxiety is triggered.
- Create a list of how God has been faithful in the past. Keep reviewing it for encouragement in present needs.
- If you underline in your Bible (and you should), read through, looking for those passages—your jewels of encouragement. Center on the Psalms.
- Increase the time you spend in prayer.
- Study Romans 8:26–27. How does the Holy Spirit help with our worry?

Resources

- *Anger, Anxiety, and Fear* (booklet). Stuart Scott. Focus.
- *Anxiety: Anatomy and Cure* (booklet). Robert Kellerman. P&R.
- *God's Attributes: Rest for Life's Struggles* (booklet). Brad Hambrick. P&R.
- *Overcoming Fear, Worry, and Anxiety.* Elyse Fitzpatrick. Harvest House.
- *Running Scared: Fear, Worry, and the God of Rest.* Ed Welch. New Growth.

Depression

See also **Aging, Disappointment, Grief, Self-Worth, Trials**

Depression is a loss of hope, one of the most overwhelming and painful struggles a couple can face. Great patience is required to help your spouse through this time. Jesus assured us that his truth will make us free (John 8:32). He promised that he would never leave us, that he would not forsake us (Hebrews 13:5). We can depend on him and his Word for help as we work through this journey.

1. **God understands our feelings of hopelessness and despair.**

    Psalm 38:9 O Lord, all my longing is before you; my sighing is not hidden from you. (ESV)

    Psalm 9:12 God remembers those who suffer; he does not forget their cry. (GNT)

    Job 23:8–10 Behold, I go forward, but he is not there, and backward, but I do not perceive him; on the left hand when he is working, I do not behold him; he turns to the right hand, but I do not see him. But he knows the way that I take; when he has tried me, I shall come out as gold. (ESV)

    Matthew 26:38 Then he said to them, "My soul is overwhelmed with sorrow to the point of death. Stay here and keep watch with me." (NIV)

2. **Individuals in the Bible experienced the weight and overwhelming nature of depression.**

    1 Kings 19:4, 13–14 He himself [Elijah] went a day's journey into the wilderness and came and sat down under a broom tree. And he asked that he might die, saying, "It is enough; now, O Lord, take away my life, for I am no better than my fathers."... Behold, there came a voice to him and said, "What are you doing here, Elijah?" He said, "I have been very jealous for the LORD, the God of hosts. For the people of Israel have forsaken your covenant, thrown down your altars, and killed your prophets with the sword, and I, even I only, am left, and they seek my life, to take it away." (ESV)

Proverbs 18:14 The spirit of a man can endure his sickness, but as for a broken spirit who can bear it? (NASB)

Psalm 69:1–3 Save me, O God, for the waters have threatened my life. I have sunk in deep mire, and there is no foothold; I have come into deep waters, and a flood overflows me. I am weary with my crying; my throat is parched; my eyes fail while I wait for my God. (NASB)

Psalm 6:6–7 I am weary with my moaning; every night I flood my bed with tears; I drench my couch with my weeping. My eye wastes away because of grief; it grows weak because of all my foes. (ESV)

Psalm 5:1–3 Listen to my words, LORD, consider my lament. Hear my cry for help, my King and my God, for to you I pray. In the morning, LORD, you hear my voice; in the morning I lay my requests before you and wait expectantly. (NIV)

Consider Job 19:7–29; Jeremiah 20:7–18.

3. **God is available to keep us from sinking further into depression.**

Psalm 42:11 Why are you cast down, O my soul, and why are you in turmoil within me? Hope in God; for I shall again praise him, my salvation and my God. (ESV)

Psalm 69:13–15 But as for me, my prayer is to you, O LORD. At an acceptable time, O God, in the abundance of your steadfast love answer me in your saving faithfulness. Deliver me from sinking in the mire; let me be delivered from my enemies and from the deep waters. Let not the flood sweep over me, or the deep swallow me up, or the pit close its mouth over me. (ESV)

Isaiah 43:1–3 But now thus says the LORD, he who created you, O Jacob, he who formed you, O Israel: "Fear not, for I have redeemed you; I have called you by name, you are mine. When you pass through the waters, I will be with you; and through the rivers, they shall not overwhelm you; when you walk through fire you shall not be burned, and the flame shall not consume you. For I am the Lord your God, the Holy One of Israel, your Savior." (ESV)

Psalm 16:8; 32:5–8

4. **God has not forgotten us. He will help us to move toward hope. He is our refuge, our rock, our strength.**

Isaiah 44:21 Remember these things, O Jacob, and Israel, for you are My servant; I have formed you, you are My servant, O Israel, you will not be forgotten by Me. (NASB)

Psalm 9:18 For the needy shall not always be forgotten, and the hope of the poor shall not perish forever. (ESV)

Psalm 43:5 Why am I discouraged? Why is my heart so sad? I will put my hope in God! I will praise him again—my Savior and my God! (NLT)

Psalm 9:9 The Lord is a stronghold for the oppressed, a stronghold in times of trouble. (ESV)

Psalm 18:2–6 The Lord is my rock, my fortress, and my savior; my God is my rock, in whom I find protection. He is my shield, the power that saves me, and my place of safety. I called on the Lord, who is worthy of praise, and he saved me from my enemies. The ropes of death entangled me; floods of destruction swept over me. The grave wrapped its ropes around me; death laid a trap in my path. But in my distress I cried out to the Lord; yes, I prayed to my God for help. He heard me from his sanctuary; my cry to him reached his ears. (NLT)

Psalm 18:28–29 You, O Lord, keep my lamp burning; my God turns my darkness into light. With your help I can advance against a troop; with my God I can scale a wall. (NIV)

Psalm 37:23–24 The steps of a man are established by the Lord, when he delights in his way; though he fall, he shall not be cast headlong, for the Lord upholds his hand. (ESV)

Psalm 138:8 You will do everything you have promised; Lord, your love is eternal. Complete the work that you have begun. (GNT)

Nahum 1:7 The Lord is good, a stronghold in the day of trouble; he knows those who take refuge in him. (ESV)

2 Corinthians 4:16 Therefore we do not lose heart. Though outwardly we are wasting away, yet inwardly we are being renewed day by day. (NIV)

Psalm 34; 46; 55:22; Jeremiah 29:11–12; Hebrews 12:2

5. **Essential for healing is prayer and the monitoring of our thinking. Sound theology leads to sound thinking.**

   Philippians 4:6–8 Don't worry about anything; instead, pray about everything. Tell God what you need, and thank him for all he has done. Then you will experience God's peace, which exceeds anything we can understand. His peace will guard your hearts and minds as you live in Christ Jesus. And now, dear brothers and sisters, one final thing. Fix your thoughts on what is true, and honorable, and right, and pure, and lovely, and admirable. Think about things that are excellent and worthy of praise. (NLT)

6. **If sin is involved in this depression, then repentance and confession must take place for the healing process to begin.**

   Psalm 32:3–5 For when I kept silent, my bones wasted away through my groaning all day long. For day and night your hand was heavy upon me; my strength was dried up as by the heat of summer. I acknowledged my sin to you, and I did not cover my iniquity; I said, "I will confess my transgressions to the Lord," and you forgave the iniquity of my sin. (ESV)

   Psalm 25:17–18 The troubles of my heart are enlarged; bring me out of my distresses. Consider my affliction and my trouble, and forgive all my sins. (ESV)

   Psalm 51

Practical Steps

- See your physician for a physical. Ask about blood tests for vitamin D, vitamin B-12, thyroid, etc. This will determine if there is an organic origin for the problem.

- If your spouse is struggling with depression, you need to patiently help them, gently speaking truth, reminding them of God's Word and your love for them. They must be given hope.
- As a couple, pray together often. Be open about your struggles. Don't give up on each other; ask God to give you the stamina you need to keep on helping the other.
- Recognize the enemy's lies—"You'll never get better; there is no hope"—for what they are. Focus on the truth of God's Word.
- Recognize that our enemy has schemes for our destruction. Study carefully Ephesians 6:10–18. Read daily Psalm 27 and 37.
- Exercise frequently. Strenuous physical activity is a great reducer of depression. Plan for thirty minutes, at least three times a week. Begin by walking.
- Share struggles with other couples, strong believers, who can provide objectivity.
- Get involved in helping others. Volunteer at a crisis pregnancy center, serve at a soup kitchen, mentor a young person, etc.

Resources

- "Depression" in *Feelings and Faith: Cultivating Godly Emotions in the Christian Life*. Brian Borgman. Crossway.
- *Depression: Looking Up from the Stubborn Darkness*. Ed Welch. New Growth.
- *God: As He Longs for You to See Him*. Chip Ingram. Baker.
- *Out of the Blues: Dealing with the Blues of Depression and Loneliness*. Wayne Mack. Focus.
- *Spiritual Depression: Its Causes and Cures*. Martin Lloyd-Jones. Eerdmans.
- *When the Darkness Will Not Lift*. John Piper. Crossway.

Disappointment

See also **Anxiety, Contentment, Depression, Failure, Trials**

Life is full of challenges and frustrations; married life has its share. Nothing is perfect in life "under the sun" (Eccles. 9:9). Disappointment is the feeling of loss or failure because our expectations, hopes, or dreams have not been met. As always, God's Word has the answers.

1. **God is in charge of the events of our lives and allows only what is for our ultimate good. We may not understand it, but we can trust him.**

   Proverbs 19:21 Many are the plans in the mind of a man, but it is the purpose of the Lord that will stand. (ESV)

   Isaiah 25:1 Lord, you are my God; I will honor you and praise your name. You have done amazing things; you have faithfully carried out the plans you made long ago. (GNT)

   Jeremiah 29:11–13 "For I know the plans I have for you," says the Lord. "They are plans for good and not for disaster, to give you a future and a hope. In those days when you pray, I will listen. If you look for me wholeheartedly, you will find me." (NLT)

   James 1:2–5 Dear brothers and sisters, when troubles of any kind come your way, consider it an opportunity for great joy. For you know that when your faith is tested, your endurance has a chance to grow. So let it grow, for when your endurance is fully developed, you will be perfect and complete, needing nothing. If you need wisdom, ask our generous God, and he will give it to you. He will not rebuke you for asking. (NLT)

2. **Even close and trusted friends (including our spouse) may disappoint us at times.**

   Psalm 41:9 Even my close friend, someone I trusted, one who shared my bread, has turned against me. (NIV)

   Psalm 55:12–14 If an enemy were insulting me, I could endure it; if a foe were rising against me, I could hide. But it is you, a man like myself, my companion, my close friend, with whom I once enjoyed sweet fellowship at the house of God, as we walked about among the worshipers. (NIV)

   Jeremiah 20:10 For I hear many whispering. Terror is on every side! "Denounce him! Let us denounce him!" say all my close friends, watching for my fall. "Perhaps he will be deceived; then we can overcome him and take our revenge on him." (ESV)

3. **God's silence does not mean his absence. He knows and cares about our feelings. He is always present, though our awareness is limited.**

   Psalm 34:18 The Lord is near to the brokenhearted and saves those who are crushed in spirit. (NASB)

   Psalm 56:8 You keep track of all my sorrows. You have collected all my tears in your bottle. You have recorded each one in your book. (NLT)

   Job 23:8–10 Behold, I go forward but He is not there, and backward, but I cannot perceive Him; when He acts on the left, I cannot behold Him; He turns on the right, I cannot see Him. But He knows the way I take; when He has tried me, I shall come forth as gold. (NASB)

   Psalm 37:24

4. **Writers in the psalms honestly voiced their disappointments to God. We can do the same.**

   Psalm 102:1–4 Hear my prayer, O Lord; let my cry come to you! Do not hide your face from me in the day of my distress! Incline your ear to me; answer me speedily in the day when I call! For my days pass away like smoke, and my bones burn like a furnace. My heart is struck down like grass and has withered; I forget to eat my bread. (ESV)

Psalm 13:1–2 How long, O Lord? Will you forget me forever? How long will you hide your face from me? How long must I take counsel in my soul and have sorrow in my heart all the day? How long shall my enemy be exalted over me? (ESV)

Psalm 22:1–2 My God, my God, why have you forsaken me? Why are you so far from saving me, from the words of my groaning? O my God, I cry by day, but you do not answer, and by night, but I find no rest. (ESV)

5. **Faith in the Lord Jesus will never disappoint. He was sent to save and to set us free.**

Luke 4:17–18, 21 And the scroll of the prophet Isaiah was given to him. He unrolled the scroll and found the place where it was written, "The Spirit of the Lord is upon me, because he has anointed me to proclaim good news to the poor. He has sent me to proclaim liberty to the captives and recovering of sight to the blind, to set at liberty those who are oppressed.". . . And he began to say to them, "Today this Scripture has been fulfilled in your hearing." (ESV)

Romans 5:1–5 Therefore, having been justified by faith, we have peace with God through our Lord Jesus Christ, through whom also we have obtained our introduction by faith into this grace in which we stand; and we exult in hope of the glory of God. And not only this, but we also exult in our tribulations, knowing that tribulation brings about perseverance; and perseverance, proven character; and proven character, hope; and hope does not disappoint, because the love of God has been poured out within our hearts through the Holy Spirit who was given to us. (NASB)

Romans 10:11 The scripture says, "Whoever believes in him will not be disappointed." (GNT)

6. **God will provide relief from disappointment. He sends deliverance, peace, and healing. It may not be in the way we expect, but he does not fail.**

Psalm 22:5 To You they cried out and were delivered; in You they trusted and were not disappointed. (NASB)

Psalm 147:3 He heals the brokenhearted and binds up their wounds. (NASB)

Ecclesiastes 3:11 Yet God has made everything beautiful for its own time. He has planted eternity in the human heart, but even so, people cannot see the whole scope of God's work from beginning to end. (NLT)

Isaiah 49:23 Then you will know that I am the Lord; no one who waits for my help will be disappointed. (GNT)

John 14:1, 27 Do not let your hearts be troubled. You believe in God; believe also in me. . . . Peace I leave with you; my peace I give you. I do not give to you as the world gives. Do not let your hearts be troubled and do not be afraid. (NIV)

7. **Husbands and wives must learn to bear each other's burdens through encouragement, prayer, and sharing. Support from other committed believers is also helpful and is God's design.**

Galatians 6:2 Carry each other's burdens, and in this way you will fulfill the law of Christ. (NIV)

Romans 15:1–2 We who are strong in the faith ought to help the weak to carry their burdens. We should not please ourselves. Instead, we should all please our brothers for their own good, in order to build them up in the faith. (GNT)

8. **Satan will use disappointment to bring defeat. Be strong for each other in not letting that happen. Know that his lies will undermine our confidence in God.**

1 Peter 5:7–9 Therefore humble yourselves. . . . casting all your anxiety on Him, because He cares for you. Be of sober spirit, be on the alert. Your adversary, the devil, prowls around like a roaring lion, seeking someone to devour. But resist him, firm in your faith, knowing that the same experiences of suffering are being accomplished by your brethren who are in the world. (NASB)

John 8:44; Ephesians 6:10–18

9. **If you as a couple are going through disappointing times, know that God can use those events to help others who have similar hurts. Look for those opportunities.**

   2 Corinthians 1:3–4 Let us give thanks to the God and Father of our Lord Jesus Christ, the merciful Father, the God from whom all help comes! He helps us in all our troubles, so that we are able to help others who have all kinds of troubles, using the same help that we ourselves have received from God. (GNT)

10. **Whatever circumstances we must endure, it is good to know that God will be glorified through them and give us the courage to face them.**

    2 Corinthians 12:9–10 But he said to me, "My grace is sufficient for you, for my power is made perfect in weakness." Therefore I will boast all the more gladly of my weaknesses, so that the power of Christ may rest upon me. For the sake of Christ, then, I am content with weaknesses, insults, hardships, persecutions, and calamities. For when I am weak, then I am strong. (ESV)

    Ephesians 3:20–21 Now to him who is able to do far more abundantly than all that we ask or think, according to the power at work within us, to him be glory in the church and in Christ Jesus throughout all generations, forever and ever. Amen. (ESV)

    Romans 11:36; 16:27; Philippians 4:19–20; 1 Timothy 1:17; 2 Timothy 4:18; Jude 24–25

Practical Steps

- As the spouse who is not struggling, take the initiative to find ways to bring encouragement to your disappointed husband/wife.
- Be in constant communication with each other. Don't be silent about your disappointments; keep on talking and encouraging the other.
- Research definitions for the attributes of God from the *Evangelical Dictionary of Theology* (Baker Books, 2001). List personal disappointments and compare what you have learned from the study.

- Commit to thanksgiving and thinking positively. Write Philippians 4:6–9 on cards. Post them close at hand in strategic locations—your home, office, or car.
- Memorize Psalm 34:18 and 147:3–5.

Resources

- *The Comeback: It's Not Too Late and You're Never Too Far*. Louie Giglio. Passion Publishing.
- *The Surprising Grace of Disappointment*. John Koessler. Moody.
- *When Bad Things Happen* (booklet). William Smith. New Growth.
- *When Disappointment Deceives*. Jeff Olson. RBC Ministries.
- *When Your World Falls Apart*. David Jeremiah. Nelson.

Grief

See also **Death, Depression, Disappointment, Forgiveness from God, Handling the Past, Trials**

Grief is a deep emotion of distress caused by great loss or difficulty. Sorrow is the sadness and regret that accompanies that loss. The words "if only" are often repeated. Martha and Mary both used these with Jesus after Lazarus died—see John 11:21, 32, "if only you had been here" (NLT).

1. **Sadness and sorrow are an inevitable part of our present human experience in this broken, fallen world.**

   Job 14:1–2 Man who is born of a woman is few of days and full of trouble. He comes out like a flower and withers; he flees like a shadow and continues not. (ESV)

   Psalm 31:9–10 Be gracious to me, O LORD, for I am in distress; my eye is wasted away from grief, my soul and my body also. For my life is spent with sorrow and my years with sighing; my strength has failed because of my iniquity, and my body has wasted away. (NASB)

   Psalm 6:6–7 I am weary with my sighing; every night I make my bed swim, I dissolve my couch with my tears. My eye has wasted away with grief; it has become old because of all my adversaries. (NASB)

   Genesis 3:16–19; Job 5:7; Psalm 90:10

2. **We are not alone when grief overwhelms. Consider and embrace the many metaphors (word pictures) in these passages.**

   Psalm 31:19 Oh, how abundant is your goodness, which you have stored up for those who fear you and worked for those who take refuge in you, in the sight of the children of mankind! (ESV)

Psalm 31:1–3 In you, O Lord, do I take refuge; let me never be put to shame; in your righteousness deliver me! Incline your ear to me; rescue me speedily! Be a rock of refuge for me, a strong fortress to save me! For you are my rock and my fortress; and for your name's sake you lead me and guide me. (ESV)

Psalm 28:7 The Lord is my strength and my shield; my heart trusted in Him, and I am helped; therefore my heart greatly rejoices, and with my song I will praise Him. (NKJV)

Isaiah 43:2 When you pass through the waters, I will be with you; and through the rivers, they shall not overflow you. When you walk through the fire, you shall not be burned, nor shall the flame scorch you. (NKJV)

Psalm 30:5; 55:22; 107:28–31; Nehemiah 8:10

3. **Knowing God is in control of our future comforts us in our loss of loved ones, as painful as it may be.**

Psalm 116:15 Precious in the sight of the Lord is the death of his saints. (ESV)

1 Thessalonians 4:13, 18 But we do not want you to be uninformed, brothers, about those who are asleep, that you may not grieve as others do who have no hope. . . . Therefore encourage one another with these words. (ESV)

Isaiah 25:8 He will swallow up death forever; and the Lord God will wipe away tears from all faces, and the reproach of his people he will take away from all the earth, for the Lord has spoken. (ESV)

4. **Thankfully, God understands our tears and gives strength.**

Psalm 6:8 For the Lord has heard the sound of my weeping. (ESV)

Psalm 56:8 You have kept count of my tossings; put my tears in your bottle. Are they not in your book? (ESV)

Psalm 126:5–6 Those who sow in tears shall reap with shouts of joy! He who goes out weeping, bearing the seed for sowing, shall come home with shouts of joy, bringing his sheaves with him. (ESV)

Isaiah 40:28–29 Have you not known? Have you not heard? The LORD is the everlasting God, the Creator of the ends of the earth. He does not faint or grow weary; his understanding is unsearchable. He gives power to the faint, and to him who has no might he increases strength. (ESV)

Psalm 119:28

5. **God experiences sorrow when we fail to live in obedience to his Word.**

   Ephesians 4:30–31 Do not bring sorrow to God's Holy Spirit by the way you live. Remember, he has identified you as his own, guaranteeing that you will be saved on the day of redemption. Get rid of all bitterness, rage, anger, harsh words, and slander, as well as all types of evil behavior. (NLT)

   Mark 3:5 He looked around at them angrily and was deeply saddened by their hard hearts. (NLT)

Practical Steps

- Write out your thoughts in a journal. Pray as you are writing. Be aware that God is right there reading along with you. Plead your case with him.
- Communicating with your spouse and trusted friends is crucial. Keeping thoughts inside does nothing to alleviate your grief and only makes it more intense. Tell your story, and then tell it again. Get it out in the open.
- Be aware of the time of day when grief is the most intense. Communicate this to your spouse. Find other strong believers who can support you during this time.
- Spend consistent time in the Psalms, especially 32, 34, 37, 42, 46, 91, 107, and 145.
- Exercise daily; practice healthy eating. Both are strong assets for emotional health.
- Study and meditate on these references where Jesus experienced sorrow: Luke 19:41; John 11:33–38.

Resources

- *Comforting Those Who Grieve*. Paul Tautges. DayOne.
- *Every Day is a New Shade of Blue: Comfort for Dark Days from Psalm 23*. David Roper. Discovery House.
- "The Sovereignty of God" and "The Wisdom of God" in *God: As He Longs for You to See Him*. Chip Ingram. Baker.
- *Through a Season of Grief* (devotionals). Bill Dunn. Nelson.
- *What Grievers Can Expect* (booklet). Wally Stephenson. RBP.

Trusting God

See also **Anxiety, Disappointment, Grief, Infertility**

When a married couple makes Christ the center of their marriage, their confidence has a firm foundation in Scripture. Trust is a confident reliance on that which is perceived to be firm, safe, and secure. This means that we must recognize that our self-confidence comes through God, who is the source and supply of our needs.

1. **As a couple experiences life's uncertainties, trust in self or others will prove unreliable. Ultimately, trust centers on God.**

   Psalm 118:8–9 It is better to take refuge in the Lord than to trust in man. It is better to take refuge in the Lord than to trust in princes. (NASB)

   Psalm 20:7 Some trust in chariots and some in horses, but we trust in the name of the Lord our God. (NIV)

   Jeremiah 17:5, 7–8 This is what the Lord says: "Cursed are those who put their trust in mere humans, who rely on human strength and turn their hearts away from the Lord. . . . But blessed are those who trust in the Lord and have made the Lord their hope and confidence. They are like trees planted along a riverbank, with roots that reach deep into the water. Such trees are not bothered by the heat or worried by long months of drought. Their leaves stay green, and they never stop producing fruit." (NLT)

   Psalm 40:4

2. **God is worthy of our trust. His presence in our lives is promised.**

   Psalm 9:10 And those who know your name put their trust in you, for you, O Lord, have not forsaken those who seek you. (ESV)

Deuteronomy 31:8 It is the Lord who goes before you. He will be with you; he will not leave you or forsake you. Do not fear or be dismayed. (ESV)

Joshua 1:5–9; Haggai 2:1–5; Matthew 28:20

3. **Trusting God for the unknown is a characteristic of faith.**

Hebrews 11:1 Now faith is confidence in what we hope for and assurance about what we do not see. (NIV)

Hebrews 11:6 And without faith it is impossible to please God, because anyone who comes to him must believe that he exists and that he rewards those who earnestly seek him. (NIV)

Hebrews 11:8–9 By faith Abraham, when called to go to a place he would later receive as his inheritance, obeyed and went, even though he did not know where he was going. By faith he made his home in the promised land like a stranger in a foreign country; he lived in tents, as did Isaac and Jacob, who were heirs with him of the same promise. (NIV)

Matthew 17:20 "You don't have enough faith," Jesus told them. "I tell you the truth, if you had faith even as small as a mustard seed, you could say to this mountain, 'Move from here to there,' and it would move. Nothing would be impossible." (NLT)

2 Corinthians 5:7

4. **Dependence on God must be constant, unwavering. This faith gets us through difficult and challenging experiences.**

Isaiah 26:4 Trust in the Lord forever, for the Lord God is an everlasting rock. (ESV)

Psalm 33:4–5 For the word of the Lord holds true, and we can trust everything he does. He loves whatever is just and good; the unfailing love of the Lord fills the earth. (NLT)

Job 23:8–10 Behold, I go forward but He is not there, and backward, but I cannot perceive Him; when He acts on the left, I cannot behold Him; He turns on the right, I cannot see Him. But He knows the way I take; when He has tried me, I shall come forth as gold. (NASB)

Habakkuk 3:17–18 Though the fig tree should not blossom and there be no fruit on the vines, though the yield of the olive should fail and the fields produce no food, though the flock should be cut off from the fold and there be no cattle in the stalls, yet I will exult in the LORD, I will rejoice in the God of my salvation. (NASB)

Psalm 26:1; 119:41–42

5. **Trusting God expresses confidence that his timing is perfect.**

Habakkuk 2:3 For the vision is yet for the appointed time; it hastens toward the goal and it will not fail. Though it tarries, wait for it; for it will certainly come, it will not delay. (NASB)

Psalm 130:5–6 I wait for the LORD, my soul does wait, and in His word do I hope. My soul waits for the Lord more than the watchmen for the morning; indeed, more than the watchmen for the morning. (NASB)

6. **Outcomes of a life of trust:**

Protection

Psalm 91:1–2 He who dwells in the shelter of the Most High will abide in the shadow of the Almighty. I will say to the LORD, "My refuge and my fortress, my God, in whom I trust!" (NASB)

Psalm 36:7 How precious is Your lovingkindness, O God! And the children of men take refuge in the shadow of Your wings. (NASB)

Psalm 5:11

Guidance

Psalm 143:8 Let me hear Your lovingkindness in the morning; for I trust in You; teach me the way in which I should walk; for to You I lift up my soul. (NASB)

Stability

Psalm 125:1–2 Those who trust in the LORD are as Mount Zion, which cannot be moved but abides forever. As the mountains surround Jerusalem, so the Lord surrounds His people from this time forth and forever. (NASB)

Fear Overcome

Psalm 56:2–4 My foes have trampled upon me all day long, for they are many who fight proudly against me. When I am afraid, I will put my trust in You. In God, whose word I praise, in God I have put my trust; I shall not be afraid. What can mere man do to me? (NASB)

Gladness

Psalm 64:10 The righteous man will be glad in the Lord and will take refuge in Him; and all the upright in heart will glory. (NASB)

Peace

Isaiah 26:3 You will keep him in perfect peace, whose mind is stayed on You, because he trusts in You. (NKJV)

Blessing

Psalm 84:12 O Lord of hosts, blessed is the man who trusts in You! (NKJV)

Jeremiah 17:7 Blessed is the man who trusts in the Lord, and whose hope is the Lord. (NKJV)

Confidence in the Future

Psalm 112:7 He will not be afraid of evil tidings; his heart is steadfast, trusting in the Lord. (NKJV)

Confidence in Prayer

Hebrews 4:16 Let us then with confidence draw near to the throne of grace, that we may receive mercy and find grace to help in time of need. (ESV)

Physical Limitations Overcome

Hebrews 11:11–12 By faith Sarah herself received power to conceive, even when she was past the age, since she considered him faithful who had promised. Therefore from one man, and him as good as dead, were born descendants as many as the stars of heaven and as many as the innumerable grains of sand by the seashore. (ESV)

Practical Steps

- Commit to sharing your deepest fears and uncertainties with each other. Learn to trust each other in complete honesty. Hidden fears will only complicate your relationship.
- Complete a study on *Yahweh*, *Elohim*, and *Adonai*, primary names of God in the Old Testament. Meditate on his trustworthiness as reflected in those names.
- Study "trust" from the Psalms using a concordance. List and categorize the verses that relate to your crisis situation.
- Meet with other mature Christian couples who have gone through situations where complete confidence in God was necessary. Share and pray with them.
- Select key verses from Psalm 145 to memorize. Keep them close at hand to remind you of God's faithfulness. Note especially verses 17–19.
- Memorize Proverbs 3:5–6.

Resources

- *The Attributes of God: A Journey into the Father's Heart*. A. W. Tozer. Christian Publications.
- "The Faithfulness of God" in *God: As He Longs for You to See Him*. Chip Ingram. Baker.
- *God Cannot Be Trusted (and Five Other Lies of Satan)*. Tony Evans. Moody.

- "Replacing a Doubtful Heart . . . with an Attitude of Trust" in *Lord, Change My Attitude*. James McDonald and Erwin Lutzer. Moody.
- *Trusting God: Even When Life Hurts*. Jerry Bridges. NavPress.

Self-Worth

See also **Depression, Pride, Selfishness**

How valuable are you? How valuable is your mate? You are of infinite worth, according to Scripture, and a reflection of God's very image!

1. **Both persons in the marriage relationship must embrace the truth that all self-worth is anchored in creation and that each is an image bearer of the Creator.**

   Genesis 1:27 God created man in His own image, in the image of God He created him; male and female He created them. (NASB)

   Genesis 5:1–2 In the day when God created man, He made him in the likeness of God. He created them male and female, and He blessed them and named them Man in the day when they were created. (NASB)

   Genesis 2:7; Luke 12:7; Psalm 139:13–14

2. **We must find significance first in our relationship to God, not in ourselves or in our spouse.**

   Micah 6:8 He has told you, O man, what is good; and what does the LORD require of you but to do justice, and to love kindness, and to walk humbly with your God? (ESV)

   2 Corinthians 5:17–18; 1 Peter 2:9

3. **Knowing God personally is what makes life truly meaningful, not intellect, power, or riches.**

   Jeremiah 9:23–24 Thus says the LORD: "Let not the wise man boast in his wisdom, let not the mighty man boast in his might, let not the rich man boast in his riches, but let him who boasts boast in this, that he understands and knows me, that I am the

Lord who practices steadfast love, justice, and righteousness in the earth. For in these things I delight, declares the Lord." (ESV)

Ephesians 1:18 I pray that the eyes of your heart may be enlightened in order that you may know the hope to which he has called you, the riches of his glorious inheritance in his holy people. (NIV)

Ephesians 3:17–20; Philippians 3:8–10

4. **Reliance on self can be a dangerous trap.**

Romans 12:3 For through the grace given to me I say to everyone among you not to think more highly of himself than he ought to think; but to think so as to have sound judgment, as God has allotted to each a measure of faith. (NASB)

2 Corinthians 1:8–9

Practical Steps

- Commit to being a husband or wife who thinks sacrificially, prioritizing your spouse's needs ahead of your own and working to fulfill those needs. When you are giving of yourself, it becomes less about you and more about the other person.
- Together memorize and meditate on Jeremiah 9:23–24. Consider carefully why intellect, power, and riches don't cut it for true meaning in life.
- Always be mindful that the person you married is an image bearer of God, and treat them as such.

Resources

- *Changed into His Image*. Jim Berg. BJU.
- *Christ Esteem: Where the Search for Self-Esteem Ends*. Don Matzat. Harvest House.
- "Finding the Real You" in *Lost in the Middle*. Paul Tripp. Shepherd.
- "When You Feel Like a Nobody Going Nowhere" in *Finding God When You Need Him Most*. Chip Ingram. Baker.

Abuse

See also **Anger, Conflict, Forgiving Each Other, Self-Control**

Abuse can take many forms and happen at various times in life. This topic considers abuse in marriage. For abuse in your past, or as a child, see *Quick Scripture Reference for Counseling Women* and *Quick Scripture Reference for Counseling Men.*

For the Abuser

Admitting the Problem

1. **Words used harshly are abusive. Don't hide behind excuses.**

   Proverbs 9:7–8 Whoever corrects a mocker invites insults; whoever rebukes the wicked incurs abuse. Do not rebuke mockers or they will hate you; rebuke the wise and they will love you. (NIV)

   Proverbs 18:21 The tongue can bring death or life; those who love to talk will reap the consequences. (NLT)

   Proverbs 21:24 The proud and arrogant person—"Mocker" is his name—behaves with insolent fury. (NIV)

   Proverbs 17:5; Galatians 5:15

2. **Acknowledge and repent of your sin.**

   1 John 1:8–10 If we say we have no sin, we deceive ourselves, and the truth is not in us. If we confess our sins, he is faithful and just to forgive us our sins and to cleanse us from all unrighteousness. If we say we have not sinned, we make him a liar, and his word is not in us. (ESV)

   Matthew 5:23–24

Making a Change

1. **Seek help and accountability from strong, mature believers.**

   Galatians 6:1–3 Brothers, if anyone is caught in any transgression, you who are spiritual should restore him in a spirit of gentleness. Keep watch on yourself, lest you too be tempted. Bear one another's burdens, and so fulfill the law of Christ. For if anyone thinks he is something, when he is nothing, he deceives himself. (ESV)

2. **Stop blaming your spouse for the abuse. She/he did not make you do it! Learn to state with conviction, "I have sinned!"**

   1 Samuel 15:24; 2 Samuel 12:13; 24:10; Psalm 51; Luke 18:13

3. **Rid yourself of abusive language.**

   Ephesians 4:29–32 Let no corrupting talk come out of your mouths, but only such as is good for building up, as fits the occasion, that it may give grace to those who hear. And do not grieve the Holy Spirit of God, by whom you were sealed for the day of redemption. Let all bitterness and wrath and anger and clamor and slander be put away from you, along with all malice. Be kind to one another, tenderhearted, forgiving one another, as God in Christ forgave you. (ESV)
   Colossians 3:8

4. **Note the abusive behavior included in these lists of sins.**

   2 Timothy 3:1–5 But mark this: There will be terrible times in the last days. People will be lovers of themselves, lovers of money, boastful, proud, abusive, disobedient to their parents, ungrateful, unholy, without love, unforgiving, slanderous, without self-control, brutal, not lovers of the good, treacherous, rash, conceited, lovers of pleasure rather than lovers of God—having a form of godliness but denying its power. (NIV)

   Galatians 5:19–20 When you follow the desires of your sinful nature, the results are very clear: sexual immorality, impurity, lustful pleasures, idolatry, sorcery, hostility, quarreling, jealousy, outbursts of anger. (NLT)

5. **Depend on the Holy Spirit. Seek his filling and control over your life.**

Galatians 5:16, 22–23 But I say, walk by the Spirit, and you will not gratify the desires of the flesh. . . . But the fruit of the Spirit is love, joy, peace, patience, kindness, goodness, faithfulness, gentleness, self-control; against such things there is no law. (ESV)

Ephesians 5:18

6. **Begin to rekindle a kind and gentle love for your spouse.**

1 Corinthians 13:4–7 Love is patient and kind; love does not envy or boast; it is not arrogant or rude. It does not insist on its own way; it is not irritable or resentful; it does not rejoice at wrongdoing, but rejoices with the truth. Love bears all things, believes all things, hopes all things, endures all things. (ESV)

To the Abused

Going through It

1. **Although we do not know when or how God will rescue us, we do know he will provide the strength we need.**

2 Corinthians 12:9–10 But he said to me, "My grace is sufficient for you, for my power is made perfect in weakness." Therefore I will boast all the more gladly about my weaknesses, so that Christ's power may rest on me. That is why, for Christ's sake, I delight in weaknesses, in insults, in hardships, in persecutions, in difficulties. For when I am weak, then I am strong. (NIV)

Psalm 31:4 You will pull me out of the net which they have secretly laid for me, for You are my strength. (NASB)

Isaiah 40:27–31; Philippians 4:6–8

2. **God is our refuge, our strong protector.**

Psalm 17:8–9 Guard me as you would guard your own eyes. Hide me in the shadow of your wings. Protect me from wicked people who attack me, from murderous enemies who surround me. (NLT)

Psalm 62:7 My victory and honor come from God alone. He is my refuge, a rock where no enemy can reach me. (NLT)

Isaiah 25:4 But you are a tower of refuge to the poor, O Lord, a tower of refuge to the needy in distress. You are a refuge from the storm and a shelter from the heat. For the oppressive acts of ruthless people are like a storm beating against a wall. (NLT)

Psalm 46; 61:3

3. **We can hope in a future day when God will redeem all things and there will be no more pain.**

Revelation 21:1–5 Then I saw a new heaven and a new earth, for the first heaven and the first earth had passed away, and the sea was no more. And I saw the holy city, new Jerusalem, coming down out of heaven from God, prepared as a bride adorned for her husband. And I heard a loud voice from the throne saying, "Behold, the dwelling place of God is with man. He will dwell with them, and they will be his people, and God himself will be with them as their God. He will wipe away every tear from their eyes, and death shall be no more, neither shall there be mourning nor crying nor pain anymore, for the former things have passed away." (ESV)

Getting Help

1. **Jesus understands the experience of abuse and will supply mercy and grace.**

Luke 23:39 One of the criminals who were hanged there was hurling abuse at Him, saying, "Are You not the Christ? Save Yourself and us!" (NASB)

Psalm 22:7–8 Everyone who sees me mocks me. They sneer and shake their heads, saying, "Is this the one who relies on the Lord? Then let the Lord save him!" (NLT)

Hebrews 4:15–16 For we do not have a high priest who is unable to sympathize with our weaknesses, but one who in every respect has been tempted as we are, yet without sin. Let us then with confidence draw near to the throne of grace, that we may receive mercy and find grace to help in time of need. (ESV)

Isaiah 53:5–6; Matthew 27:39

2. **When we feel alone, God is there, and we can call on him.**

Zephaniah 3:17 The LORD your God is with you, the Mighty Warrior who saves. He will take great delight in you; in his love he will no longer rebuke you, but will rejoice over you with singing. (NIV)

Psalm 142:1–7 I cry out to the LORD; I plead for the LORD's mercy. I pour out my complaints before him and tell him all my troubles. When I am overwhelmed, you alone know the way I should turn. Wherever I go, my enemies have set traps for me. I look for someone to come and help me, but no one gives me a passing thought! No one will help me; no one cares a bit what happens to me. Then I pray to you, O LORD. I say, "You are my place of refuge. You are all I really want in life. Hear my cry, for I am very low. Rescue me from my persecutors, for they are too strong for me. Bring me out of prison so I can thank you. The godly will crowd around me, for you are good to me." (NLT)

Psalm 59:1

3. **Seek help from those who could be burden bearers with you—church leaders, family, Christian friends, government agencies.**

Galatians 6:2 Bear one another's burdens, and so fulfill the law of Christ. (ESV)

Acts 20:35 In everything I showed you that by working hard in this manner you must help the weak and remember the words of the Lord Jesus, that He Himself said, "It is more blessed to give than to receive." (NASB) (The context is Paul writing to the elders of the church at Ephesus.)

Psalm 82:3–4 Give justice to the weak and the fatherless; maintain the right of the afflicted and the destitute. Rescue the weak and the needy; deliver them from the hand of the wicked. (ESV) (The context is Asaph speaking to the judges of Israel.)

4. **David prayed for safety from abusers—we can do the same.**

Psalm 140:1–6 O Lord, rescue me from evil people. Protect me from those who are violent, those who plot evil in their hearts and stir up trouble all day long. Their tongues sting like a snake; the venom of a viper drips from their lips. O Lord, keep me out of the hands of the wicked. Protect me from those who are violent, for they are plotting against me. The proud have set a trap to catch me; they have stretched out a net; they have placed traps all along the way. I said to the Lord, "You are my God!" Listen, O Lord, to my cries for mercy! (NLT)

Psalm 61:1–4

Practical Steps

To the Abuser

- Stop blaming everyone else. You are the problem!
- Abuse in any form is never acceptable.
- Admit the problem and seek strong, biblical counseling.
- Get down on your knees, and pray David's prayer in Psalm 51!
- Be accountable to a strong brother or sister in Christ.
- Be alert for the triggers that bring a sinful response, and take steps to move away from the situation—into another room or out of the house.

To the Abused

- Create a safety plan with a trusted individual—emergency phone numbers, safe house, money, etc.
- Keep a record of events, what was said and done.
- Separate yourself from the situation. Seek out a shelter or a friend's home; get a restraining order.
- Start a healing journal of prayers, Scripture, and forgiveness.
- It would be beneficial to see a physician.

Resources

- *Abused*. Richard and Lois Klempel. Fairway.
- *Emotionally Destructive Relationships*. Leslie Vernick. Harvest House.
- "The Meaning of Man" and "Women" in *The Strength of a Man*. David Roper. Discovery House.
- *Rid of My Disgrace*. Justin and Lindsey Holcomb. Crossway.

Life Challenges

Everyone experiences the "ups and downs" of life. *Good*, *bad*, *exciting*, *beautiful*, *challenging*, and *eventful* are all words that come to mind. That "stuff happens" in marriage is a given. Difficult times and transition times are inevitable. Foundational to living joyfully and productively is the assurance that God is over all, and his presence and care will get us through every season of marriage. The following topics bring Scripture to bear on dealing with key issues.

Infertility

See also **Depression, Disappointment, Grief, Trials, Trusting God**

For most married couples, having children is a much anticipated part of the dreams they share together. Infertility, with all its emotional and physical struggles, can be shattering and one of the most difficult experiences to go through. Where is God in all of this?

1. **Never lose hope in God's faithfulness in spite of deep sorrow.**

   Lamentations 3:19–26 Remember my affliction and my wanderings, the wormwood and the gall! My soul continually remembers it and is bowed down within me. But this I call to mind, and therefore I have hope: The steadfast love of the Lord never ceases; his mercies never come to an end; they are new every morning; great is your faithfulness. "The Lord is my portion," says my soul, "therefore I will hope in him." The Lord is good to those who wait for him, to the soul who seeks him. It is good that one should wait quietly for the salvation of the Lord. (ESV)

2. **God understands and has compassion for all of our needs, including the deep pain of barrenness.**

   Isaiah 54:1 "Shout for joy, O barren one, you who have borne no child; break forth into joyful shouting and cry aloud, you who have not travailed; for the sons of the desolate one will be more numerous than the sons of the married woman," says the Lord. (NASB)

   Psalm 94:19 When doubts filled my mind, your comfort gave me renewed hope and cheer. (NLT)

   Psalm 69:1–3 Save me, O God, for the waters have threatened my life. I have sunk in deep mire, and there is no foothold; I have come into deep waters, and a flood overflows me. I am weary with my crying; my throat is parched; my eyes fail while I wait for my God. (NASB)

Psalm 142:3 When my spirit grows faint within me, it is you who watch over my way. (NIV)

Proverbs 30:15–16 There are three things that are never satisfied—no, four that never say, "Enough!": the grave, the barren womb, the thirsty desert, the blazing fire. (NLT)

3. **As difficult as it is, confidence needs to be placed fully in God, trusting him for the possibility of a future without children.**

Habakkuk 3:17–19 Though the fig tree should not blossom and there be no fruit on the vines, though the yield of the olive should fail and the fields produce no food, though the flock should be cut off from the fold and there be no cattle in the stalls, yet I will exult in the Lord, I will rejoice in the God of my salvation. The Lord God is my strength, and He has made my feet like hinds' feet, and makes me walk on my high places. (NASB)

2 Corinthians 12:9 And He has said to me, "My grace is sufficient for you, for power is perfected in weakness." Most gladly, therefore, I will rather boast about my weaknesses, so that the power of Christ may dwell in me. (NASB)

Job 13:15 Though he slay me, I will hope in him. (ESV)

Isaiah 40:29 He gives strength to the weary, and to him who lacks might He increases power. (NASB)

Isaiah 55:8–9 "For My thoughts are not your thoughts, nor are your ways My ways," declares the Lord. "For as the heavens are higher than the earth, so are My ways higher than your ways and My thoughts than your thoughts." (NASB)

4. **Consider these biblical examples showing pain, desperation, and prayers for children.**

Sarah

Genesis 11:30; 16:1

Rebekah
Genesis 25:21

Rachel
Genesis 30:1

Samson's mother
Judges 13:2

Hannah
1 Samuel 1:10; 2:5

Elizabeth
Luke 1

Practical Steps

- Study carefully each of the "See also" topics listed above. Each contains much biblical truth for painful experiences such as infertility.
- Explore the many medical possibilities for infertility treatment.
- How did each of the women mentioned above handle their barrenness? What did God do through their pain?
- Research adoption or foster care. Perhaps helping other children is God's plan for you.
- Be open to encouragement from others—discuss, pray. Avoid keeping your hurt inside and alone.

Resources

- "Faith: When God Seems Absent, Indifferent, or Even Hostile" in *Reaching for the Invisible God*. Philip Yancey. Zondervan.
- "Knowing When to Keep Praying," in *A Journey to Victorious Praying*. Bill Thrasher. Moody.

- *Moments for Couples Who Long for Children*. Ginger Garrett. NavPress.
- *Morning Will Come*. Sandy Day. Focus.
- *When the Cradle Is Empty*. John and Sylvia Van Regenmorter. Tyndale.

Contraception

See also **Anxiety, Decision Making, Disappointment, Finances**

While Scripture does not specifically speak to this issue, these principles do apply.

1. **Scripture is clear that children are blessings and gifts from God.**

   Psalm 127:3–5 Behold, children are a gift of the Lord, the fruit of the womb is a reward. Like arrows in the hand of a warrior, so are the children of one's youth. How blessed is the man whose quiver is full of them; they will not be ashamed when they speak with their enemies in the gate. (NASB)

   Proverbs 17:6 Children's children are a crown to the aged, and parents are the pride of their children. (NIV)

   Psalm 128:3–4 Your wife shall be like a fruitful vine in the very heart of your house, your children like olive plants all around your table. Behold, thus shall the man be blessed who fears the Lord. (NKJV)

   Matthew 18:5 And whoever receives one such child in My name receives Me. (NASB)

2. **As with any major decision, you need to seek God's wisdom and guidance. Important decisions need to be made prayerfully according to his will.**

   James 1:5 If any of you lacks wisdom, you should ask God, who gives generously to all without finding fault, and it will be given to you. (NIV)

   Ephesians 5:15–17 Look carefully then how you walk, not as unwise but as wise, making the best use of the time, because the days are evil. Therefore do not be foolish, but understand what the will of the Lord is. (ESV)

Proverbs 3:5–6 Trust in the LORD with all your heart; do not depend on your own understanding. Seek his will in all you do, and he will show you which path to take. (NLT)

James 3:17 But the wisdom from above is first pure, then peaceable, gentle, open to reason, full of mercy and good fruits, impartial and sincere. (ESV)

Proverbs 2:6–7

3. **God is sovereign; he will act according to his plan, birth control or no birth control.**

Job 42:2 I know that you can do all things, and that no purpose of yours can be thwarted. (ESV)

Isaiah 43:13 Even from eternity I am He, and there is none who can deliver out of My hand; I act and who can reverse it? (NASB)

Isaiah 14:27 For the LORD of hosts has planned, and who can frustrate it? And as for His stretched-out hand, who can turn it back? (NASB)

Ephesians 1:11 In him we were also chosen, having been predestined according to the plan of him who works out everything in conformity with the purpose of his will. (NIV)

Jeremiah 32:17, 27

4. **Any birth control that destroys the newly conceived embryo is wrong and is unacceptable (some birth control pills, some intrauterine devices). That embryo is a real person from the instant of conception as God begins to form him or her in the womb.**

Isaiah 44:24 Thus says the LORD, your Redeemer, who formed you from the womb: "I am the LORD, who made all things, who alone stretched out the heavens, who spread out the earth by myself." (ESV)

Psalm 139:13–16

Practical Steps

- If possible, see a Christian physician (pro-life) for answers to questions.

- Decisions must be made jointly, in agreement, with neither spouse forcing his or her will on the other.
- Discuss openly with your spouse, and pray together regarding the use of birth control.
- Research types of birth control. Look for conception blocking (does not allow a baby to begin). Stay away from implantation blocking (the baby is alive, but not allowed to continue).
- Evaluate your motivations for using birth control. Make sure that selfishness or self-centeredness are not a factor.
- If pregnancy does occur while on birth control, take joy in God's sovereignty.

Resources

- "Abortion" in *Culture Shock*. Chip Ingram. Baker.
- *Does the Birth Control Pill Cause Abortions?* Randy Alcorn. EPM.
- "Planning and Achieving Parenthood" in *Intended for Pleasure*. Ed and Gaye Wheat. Revell.

Abortion

See also **Anxiety, Decision Making, Materialism, Selfishness**

An unexpected pregnancy—perhaps the timing is just not right or you feel you have enough children already. One thing is certain: you are very much responsible for the continuing welfare of that baby. Scripture is clear about this issue of life from conception and that an abortion is never right, and is never the will of God. The second part of this topic deals with recovery if an abortion has occurred.

The Need to Choose Life

1. **God is actively and personally involved in the life of every unborn person, including plans for each day of his or her life.**

   Psalm 139:16 Your eyes saw my unformed substance; in your book were written, every one of them, the days that were formed for me, when as yet there was none of them. (ESV)

   Genesis 25:21–23 Isaac prayed to the LORD on behalf of his wife, because she was childless. The LORD answered his prayer, and his wife Rebekah became pregnant. The babies jostled each other within her, and she said, "Why is this happening to me?" So she went to inquire of the LORD. The LORD said to her, "Two nations are in your womb, and two peoples from within you will be separated; one people will be stronger than the other, and the older will serve the younger." (NIV)

2. **Birth is the arrival of life, not the beginning. The baby in the womb is a living human being from conception. Note the frequent use of personal pronouns in reference to this unborn baby.**

Psalm 139:13–15 For you formed my inward parts; you knitted me together in my mother's womb. I praise you, for I am fearfully and wonderfully made. Wonderful are your works; my soul knows it very well. My frame was not hidden from you, when I was being made in secret, intricately woven in the depths of the earth. (ESV)

3. **The prophets comprehended that God knew them as persons before they were born.**

Jeremiah 1:5 I knew you before I formed you in your mother's womb. Before you were born I set you apart and appointed you as my prophet to the nations. (NLT)

Isaiah 49:1 Listen to me, you islands; hear this, you distant nations: Before I was born the Lord called me; from my mother's womb he has spoken my name. (NIV)

4. **Elizabeth's unborn baby was aware of Jesus, Mary's unborn baby. Through a unique situation (the God-man in the womb) evidence is provided for personhood in the womb.**

Luke 1:44 As soon as the sound of your greeting reached my ears, the baby in my womb leaped for joy. (NIV) (See vv. 39–44.)

5. **God's people must work to prevent abortions.**

Proverbs 24:11–12 Rescue those who are being taken away to death; hold back those who are stumbling to the slaughter. If you say, "Behold, we did not know this," does not he who weighs the heart perceive it? Does not he who keeps watch over your soul know it, and will he not repay man according to his work? (ESV)

6. **Self-will to follow what we want, rather than what God wants, is sin and leads to heartache and trouble.**

 Psalm 19:13 Keep your servant from deliberate sins! Don't let them control me. Then I will be free of guilt and innocent of great sin. (NLT)

 Proverbs 14:12 There is a way that seems right to a man, but its end is the way to death. (ESV)

 Proverbs 16:2 People may be pure in their own eyes, but the Lord examines their motives. (NLT)

7. **Our actions are not hidden from God.**

 2 Chronicles 16:9 The eyes of the Lord search the whole earth in order to strengthen those whose hearts are fully committed to him. (NLT)

 Psalm 139:7–12 I can never escape from your Spirit! I can never get away from your presence! If I go up to heaven, you are there; if I go down to the grave, you are there. If I ride the wings of the morning, if I dwell by the farthest oceans, even there your hand will guide me, and your strength will support me. I could ask the darkness to hide me and the light around me to become night—but even in darkness I cannot hide from you. To you the night shines as bright as day. (NLT)

 Hebrews 4:13 Nothing in all creation is hidden from God's sight. Everything is uncovered and laid bare before the eyes of him to whom we must give account. (NIV)

8. **Children are a gift from God, no matter the circumstances of their conception.**

 Psalm 127:3–4 Behold, children are a gift of the Lord, the fruit of the womb is a reward. Like arrows in the hand of a warrior, so are the children of one's youth. (NASB)

9. **Our bodies, our very lives, belong not to us but to God.**

 1 Corinthians 6:19–20 Don't you realize that your body is the temple of the Holy Spirit, who lives in you and was given to you by God? You do not belong to yourself, for God bought you with a high price. So you must honor God with your body. (NLT)

Romans 12:1–2 And so, dear brothers and sisters, I plead with you to give your bodies to God because of all he has done for you. Let them be a living and holy sacrifice—the kind he will find acceptable. This is truly the way to worship him. Don't copy the behavior and customs of this world, but let God transform you into a new person by changing the way you think. Then you will learn to know God's will for you, which is good and pleasing and perfect. (NLT)

2 Corinthians 6:16

10. **Choose life! Escaping from a pregnancy and its consequences is selfishness and sin. Choosing God's way might be difficult, but is a decision that leads to life and peace and one of no regret.**

Romans 8:5–6 Those who live according to the flesh have their minds set on what the flesh desires; but those who live in accordance with the Spirit have their minds set on what the Spirit desires. The mind governed by the flesh is death, but the mind governed by the Spirit is life and peace. (NIV)

Philippians 1:9–10 And this is my prayer: that your love may abound more and more in knowledge and depth of insight, so that you may be able to discern what is best and may be pure and blameless for the day of Christ. (NIV)

Joshua 24:14–15 Now fear the Lord and serve him with all faithfulness. Throw away the gods your ancestors worshiped beyond the Euphrates River and in Egypt, and serve the Lord. But if serving the Lord seems undesirable to you, then choose for yourselves this day whom you will serve. . . . But as for me and my household, we will serve the Lord. (NIV) (Think present-day gods.)

Joshua 1:9

Practical Steps

- You must understand the baby's development. An ultrasound is crucial.
- Memorize Psalm 139:16; post it on a card and review it often.

- Memorize Isaiah 43:1–2.
- Consider having someone adopt your baby if caring for this child would be too much for you. Give your baby life, rather than death.

Resources

- *Pro-life Answers to Pro-choice Arguments*. Randy Alcorn. Multnomah.

If an Abortion Has Occurred

See also **Confession, Forgiveness from God, Grief, Handling the Past**

1. **Forgiveness from God is completely available.**

   1 John 1:9 If we confess our sins, he is faithful and just to forgive us our sins and to cleanse us from all unrighteousness. (ESV)

   Micah 7:18–19 Who is a God like you, pardoning iniquity and passing over transgression for the remnant of his inheritance? He does not retain his anger forever, because he delights in steadfast love. He will again have compassion on us; he will tread our iniquities underfoot. You will cast all our sins into the depths of the sea. (ESV)

   Psalm 32:5 Finally, I confessed all my sins to you and stopped trying to hide my guilt. I said to myself, "I will confess my rebellion to the Lord." And you forgave me! All my guilt is gone. (NLT)

2. **God can take our broken hearts and produce joy.**

   Psalm 51:12–15 Restore to me the joy of your salvation, and uphold me with a willing spirit. Then I will teach transgressors your ways, and sinners will return to you. Deliver me from blood guiltiness, O God, O God of my salvation, and my tongue will sing aloud of your righteousness. O Lord, open my lips, and my mouth will declare your praise. (ESV)

3. **God offers restoration and freedom.**

Psalm 40:1–3 I waited patiently for the Lord; he turned to me and heard my cry. He lifted me out of the slimy pit, out of the mud and mire; he set my feet on a rock and gave me a firm place to stand. He put a new song in my mouth, a hymn of praise to our God. Many will see and fear the Lord and put their trust in him. (NIV)

John 8:32, 36 Then you will know the truth, and the truth will set you free. . . . So if the Son sets you free, you will be free indeed. (NIV)

4. **God understands Israelites weeping for children they would never see again. He understands our grief over the loss of a baby.**

Jeremiah 31:15 Thus says the Lord: "A voice was heard in Ramah, lamentation and bitter weeping, Rachel weeping for her children, refusing to be comforted for her children, because they are no more." (NKJV)

5. **As the Israelites in captivity were not to dwell on past mistakes, we also should not dwell on the past once it is forgiven.**

Isaiah 43:18–19 Forget the former things; do not dwell on the past. See, I am doing a new thing! Now it springs up; do you not perceive it? I am making a way in the wilderness and streams in the wasteland. (NIV)

6. **When we are grieving deeply, God is our source of comfort.**

Psalm 18:1–6 I love you, Lord, my strength. The Lord is my rock, my fortress and my deliverer; my God is my rock, in whom I take refuge, my shield and the horn of my salvation, my stronghold. I called to the Lord, who is worthy of praise, and I have been saved from my enemies. The cords of death entangled me; the torrents of destruction overwhelmed me. The cords of the grave coiled around me; the snares of death confronted me. In my distress I called to the Lord; I cried to my God for help. From his temple he heard my voice; my cry came before him, into his ears. (NIV)

Isaiah 25:8 He will swallow up death forever; and the Lord GOD will wipe away tears from all faces, and the reproach of his people he will take away from all the earth, for the LORD has spoken. (ESV)

Practical Steps

- Study carefully the "Forgiveness from God" and "Grief" topics in this book.
- Look for a church with a support ministry for those grieving over having an abortion.
- Choose something special—planting a tree, a piece of jewelry, etc.—that can be a memorial, reminding you of God's forgiveness and in remembrance of your baby.

Resources

- *Healing After Abortion* (booklet). David Powlison. New Growth.
- *Her Choice to Heal: Finding Spiritual and Emotional Peace after Abortion*. Sydna Massé. Chariot Victor.
- *When the Pain Won't Go Away: Dealing with the Effects of Abortion* (booklet). RBC Ministries.

Parenting

See also **Anxiety, Decision Making, Prodigal Children, Trusting God**

So here comes that first baby! Now what? Eighteen-plus years (and really, you are never finished parenting) to do your very best to raise that little one to be a responsible and God-fearing adult. An enormous challenge!

1. **There are many scriptural values for good parenting.**

Keeping your word

Psalm 15:2, 4 He [pleases God] who walks blamelessly and does what is right and speaks truth in his heart; . . . who swears to his own hurt and does not change. (ESV)

Leviticus 19:11–12 Do not steal or cheat or lie. Do not make a promise in my name if you do not intend to keep it; that brings disgrace on my name. I am the LORD your God. (GNT)

Dealing fairly

Proverbs 21:3 Do what is right and fair; that pleases the LORD more than bringing him sacrifices. (GNT)

Psalm 106:3 There is joy for those who deal justly with others and always do what is right. (NLT)

Psalm 89:14

Listening well before speaking

Proverbs 18:13 If one gives an answer before he hears, it is his folly and shame. (ESV)

James 1:19 Understand this, my dear brothers and sisters: You must all be quick to listen, slow to speak, and slow to get angry. (NLT)

Speaking softly and carefully

Proverbs 12:18 Some people make cutting remarks, but the words of the wise bring healing. (NLT)

Proverbs 15:1–4

Loving with a humble, gentle, patient attitude

Ephesians 4:2 Always be humble and gentle. Be patient with each other, making allowance for each other's faults because of your love. (NLT)

Evidencing the fruit of the Spirit

Galatians 5:22–23 But the fruit of the Spirit is love, joy, peace, patience, kindness, goodness, faithfulness, gentleness, self-control; against such things there is no law. (NASB)

Building up with kindness, compassion, forgiveness

Ephesians 4:29–32 Let no unwholesome word proceed from your mouth, but only such a word as is good for edification according to the need of the moment, so that it will give grace to those who hear. Do not grieve the Holy Spirit of God, by whom you were sealed for the day of redemption. Let all bitterness and wrath and anger and clamor and slander be put away from you, along with all malice. Be kind to one another, tender-hearted, forgiving each other, just as God in Christ also has forgiven you. (NASB)

Expressing humility, sympathy, love

1 Peter 3:8–9

2. **Children are a blessing directly from God.**

Psalm 127:3–5 Behold, children are a heritage from the Lord, the fruit of the womb a reward. Like arrows in the hand of a warrior are the children of one's youth. Blessed is the man who fills his quiver with them! He shall not be put to shame when he speaks with his enemies in the gate. (ESV)

Genesis 33:5 He lifted his eyes and saw the women and the children, and said, "Who are these with you?" So he said, "The children whom God has graciously given your servant." (NASB)

Genesis 1:27–28; Psalm 128:3–4

3. **Your love and provision for your children will model that of the heavenly Father.**

Matthew 7:9–11 You parents—if your children ask for a loaf of bread, do you give them a stone instead? Or if they ask for a fish, do you give them a snake? Of course not! So if you sinful people know how to give good gifts to your children, how much more will your heavenly Father give good gifts to those who ask him. (NLT)

Romans 8:32 He who did not spare his own Son but gave him up for us all, how will he not also with him graciously give us all things? (ESV)

Psalm 84:11

4. **Parents are to be intentional and focused, taking advantage of every teachable moment.**

Deuteronomy 6:4–9 Listen, O Israel! The LORD is our God, the LORD alone. And you must love the LORD your God with all your heart, all your soul, and all your strength. And you must commit yourselves wholeheartedly to these commands that I am giving you today. Repeat them again and again to your children. Talk about them when you are at home and when you are on the road, when you are going to bed and when you are getting up. Tie them to your hands and wear them on your forehead as reminders. Write them on the doorposts of your house and on your gates. (NLT)

Joshua 4:21–23 He said to the sons of Israel, "When your children ask their fathers in time to come, saying, 'What are these stones?' then you shall inform your children, saying, 'Israel crossed this Jordan on dry ground.' For the LORD your God dried up the waters of the Jordan before you." (NASB)

Psalm 78:4–7 We will not hide these truths from our children; we will tell the next generation about the glorious deeds of the

Lord, about his power and his mighty wonders. For he issued his laws to Jacob; he gave his instructions to Israel. He commanded our ancestors to teach them to their children, so the next generation might know them—even the children not yet born—and they in turn will teach their own children. So each generation should set its hope anew on God, not forgetting his glorious miracles and obeying his commands. (NLT)

Proverbs 4:3–5 When I was a son to my father, tender and the only son in the sight of my mother, then he taught me and said to me, "Let your heart hold fast my words; keep my commandments and live; acquire wisdom! Acquire understanding! Do not forget nor turn away from the words of my mouth." (NASB)

Proverbs 22:6; Isaiah 38:19; Ephesians 6:4; 1 Thessalonians 2:11–12

5. **Children must obey their parents. Fathers and mothers must lovingly and firmly establish parental authority.**

Colossians 3:20 Children, obey your parents in everything, for this pleases the Lord. (ESV)

Ephesians 6:1–3 Children, obey your parents in the Lord, for this is right. "Honor your father and mother" (this is the first commandment with a promise), "that it may go well with you and that you may live long in the land." (ESV)

Deuteronomy 5:16

6. **Parents must use corrective discipline firmly but lovingly, fairly applied, and never to an extreme.**

Proverbs 3:11–12 My son, do not despise the Lord's discipline or be weary of his reproof, for the Lord reproves him whom he loves, as a father the son in whom he delights. (ESV)

Proverbs 29:17 Discipline your children, and they will give you peace of mind and will make your heart glad. (NLT)

Hebrews 12:9–11 Besides this, we have had earthly fathers who disciplined us and we respected them. Shall we not much more be subject to the Father of spirits and live? For they disciplined us for a short time as it seemed best to them, but he disciplines us for our good, that we may share his holiness. For the moment all discipline seems painful rather than pleasant, but later it yields the peaceful fruit of righteousness to those who have been trained by it. (ESV)

Proverbs 13:24; 19:18

7. **Fathers have specific instructions toward patience and understanding.**

   Ephesians 6:4 Fathers, do not provoke your children to anger, but bring them up in the discipline and instruction of the Lord. (NASB)

   Colossians 3:21 Fathers, do not exasperate your children, so that they will not lose heart. (NASB)

8. **Children will not always choose to walk in God's ways. Note this principle of individual accountability. Children are responsible for their own decisions, good or bad.**

   Ezekiel 18:20 The soul who sins shall die. The son shall not suffer for the iniquity of the father, nor the father suffer for the iniquity of the son. The righteousness of the righteous shall be upon himself, and the wickedness of the wicked shall be upon himself. (ESV) (The context of chapter 18 is especially important.)

   Deuteronomy 24:16

Practical Steps

- When you leave work, leave work behind. Turn off your work cell phone at home.
- Which is more important? A spotlessly clean house, or time spent with children?
- As a couple, spend time with your children. It is the best investment you can make. Evaluate that amount of time; most likely it needs to be increased.
- Plan activities with your children that they will enjoy. Be age/development conscious about what they would like to do.

- Know that our culture's view of sin and discipline is vastly different from Scripture. Resist the pressures advocating permissiveness.
- Never discipline when you are angry. Reacting too quickly is usually overreacting. Discuss with your spouse specific measures for specific offenses. Have a plan in place.
- Always keep in mind that one of your parenting goals is to prepare children to move out and be on their own when they become adults. Avoid smothering and overprotecting.
- Children should move from being dependent on you to being dependent upon God.

Resources

- *Age of Opportunity: A Biblical Guide to Parenting Teens*. Paul Tripp. P&R.
- *Everyday Talk: Talking Freely and Naturally about God with Your Children*. John A. Younts. Shepherd Press.
- *Give Them Grace: Dazzling Your Kids with the Love of Jesus* (book and CDs). Elyse Fitzpatrick. Crossway.
- *Gospel-Powered Parenting*. William P. Farley. P&R.
- *Quick Scripture Reference for Counseling Youth*. Keith and Pat Miller. Baker.
- *You Never Stop Being a Parent: Thriving in Relationship with Your Adult Children*. Jim Newheiser and Elyse Fitzpatrick. P&R.

Prodigal Children

See also **Anxiety, Disappointment, Forgiving Each Other, Trusting God**

Of all the struggles Christian parents face, having a nonbelieving child or one who as a teen or adult walks away from the Lord is among the most heartbreaking. Guilt, blame, fear, conflict, etc., are all a part of the pain. The "if only we had done this" thoughts never seem to go away. Yet, as always, knowing and applying God's Word is critical as we deal with the many issues involved.

1. **Children will not always walk in God's ways. Yet they are responsible for their own decisions, good or bad. Note this principle of individual accountability.**

   Ezekiel 18:20 The son shall not suffer for the iniquity of the father, nor the father suffer for the iniquity of the son. The righteousness of the righteous shall be upon himself, and the wickedness of the wicked shall be upon himself. (ESV) (The context of chapter 18 is especially important.)
   Deuteronomy 24:16

2. **Having a child who isn't walking with God brings terrible pain.**

   Proverbs 17:25 Foolish children bring grief to their father and bitterness to the one who gave them birth. (NLT)
   Proverbs 10:1 A wise son makes a glad father, but a foolish son is the grief of his mother. (NKJV)
   Isaiah 65:2 I have spread out My hands all day long to a rebellious people, who walk in the way which is not good, following their own thoughts. (NASB)

3. **God understands wayward children and the grief parents experience. (The context in these verses is his nation, Israel.)**

    Jeremiah 3:22 "My wayward children," says the Lord, "come back to me, and I will heal your wayward hearts." (NLT)

    Isaiah 1:2 Listen, O heavens! Pay attention, earth! This is what the Lord says: "The children I raised and cared for have rebelled against me." (NLT)

    Jeremiah 6:16 Thus says the Lord: "Stand in the ways and see, and ask for the old paths, where the good way is, and walk in it; then you will find rest for your souls. But they said, 'We will not walk in it.'" (NKJV)

4. **Couples who face this crisis must be careful to maintain a loving, understanding relationship with each other—no blame game, guilt trips, etc.**

    Psalm 19:14 Let the words of my mouth and the meditation of my heart be acceptable in your sight, O Lord, my rock and my redeemer. (ESV)

    Proverbs 19:13 A foolish child is a father's ruin, and a quarrelsome wife is like the constant dripping of a leaky roof. (NIV) (The same would apply as the genders are reversed.)

    Ephesians 5:25, 28; 1 Peter 3:7; James 3:2–12

5. **The battle with the enemy is not ours but God's.**

    2 Chronicles 20:15 And he said, "Listen, all Judah and inhabitants of Jerusalem and King Jehoshaphat: Thus says the Lord to you, 'Do not be afraid and do not be dismayed at this great horde, for the battle is not yours but God's.'" (ESV)

    Proverbs 21:31 The horse is prepared for the day of battle, but deliverance is of the Lord. (NKJV)

    Psalm 62:11–12 Once God has spoken; twice have I heard this: that power belongs to God, and that to you, O Lord, belongs steadfast love. (ESV)

    Isaiah 49:25 For thus says the Lord: "Even the captives of the mighty shall be taken, and the prey of the tyrant be rescued, for I will contend with those who contend with you, and I will save your children." (ESV)

John 16:33 These things I have spoken to you, that in Me you may have peace. In the world you will have tribulation; but be of good cheer, I have overcome the world. (NKJV)

2 Chronicles 14:11

6. **As you deal with this pain, make sure your own walk with the Lord remains vital and fresh. Do not lose your confidence in God. Live out your faith before your child.**

Galatians 6:1 Brothers and sisters, if someone is caught in a sin, you who are spiritual should restore him gently. But watch yourself, or you also may be tempted. (NIV)

James 1:2–5 Consider it all joy, my brethren, when you encounter various trials, knowing that the testing of your faith produces endurance. And let endurance have its perfect result, so that you may be perfect and complete, lacking in nothing. But if any of you lacks wisdom, let him ask of God, who gives to all generously and without reproach, and it will be given to him. (NASB)

7. **Work at keeping an open relationship and communication with your child so when God gives the opportunity, he or she may listen.**

1 Corinthians 13:4–7 Love suffers long and is kind; love does not envy; love does not parade itself, is not puffed up; does not behave rudely, does not seek its own, is not provoked, thinks no evil; does not rejoice in iniquity, but rejoices in the truth; bears all things, believes all things, hopes all things, endures all things. (NKJV)

James 5:19–20 My brothers, if anyone among you wanders from the truth and someone brings him back, let him know that whoever brings back a sinner from his wandering will save his soul from death and will cover a multitude of sins. (ESV)

Isaiah 58:7 Share your food with the hungry, and give shelter to the homeless. Give clothes to those who need them, and do not hide from relatives who need your help. (NLT)

Proverbs 29:11 Fools vent their anger, but the wise quietly hold it back. (NLT)

1 Peter 4:8 And above all things have fervent love for one another, for "love will cover a multitude of sins." (NKJV)

Galatians 5:22–23 But the fruit of the Spirit is love, joy, peace, longsuffering, kindness, goodness, faithfulness, gentleness, self-control. Against such there is no law. (NKJV)

Psalm 37:8 Cease from anger, and forsake wrath; do not fret—it only causes harm. (NKJV)

Proverbs 20:3

8. **Pray constantly for your child, not necessarily for what is wanted as a parent, but for what God wants to do in your child's life.**

1 Samuel 1:27–28 For this boy I prayed, and the Lord has given me my petition which I asked of Him. So I have also dedicated him to the Lord; as long as he lives he is dedicated to the Lord. (NASB)

Romans 8:26 In the same way the Spirit also helps our weakness; for we do not know how to pray as we should, but the Spirit Himself intercedes for us with groanings too deep for words. (NASB)

Matthew 7:7–11 Ask, and it will be given to you; seek, and you will find; knock, and it will be opened to you. For everyone who asks receives, and he who seeks finds, and to him who knocks it will be opened. Or what man is there among you who, when his son asks for a loaf, will give him a stone? Or if he asks for a fish, he will not give him a snake, will he? If you then, being evil, know how to give good gifts to your children, how much more will your Father who is in heaven give what is good to those who ask Him! (NASB)

2 Corinthians 12:8–10

9. **Have hope—God desires for your child to be restored. Anticipate what he can do.**

2 Peter 3:9 The Lord is not slow about His promise, as some count slowness, but is patient toward you, not wishing for any to perish but for all to come to repentance. (NASB)

Jeremiah 32:27 Behold, I am the Lord, the God of all flesh; is anything too difficult for Me? (NASB)

Lamentations 3:25–26 The Lord is good to those who wait for Him, to the person who seeks Him. It is good that he waits silently for the salvation of the Lord. (NASB)

Luke 15:20 So he got up and came to his father. But while he was still a long way off, his father saw him and felt compassion for him, and ran and embraced him and kissed him. (NASB)

Romans 15:13 Now may the God of hope fill you with all joy and peace in believing, so that you will abound in hope by the power of the Holy Spirit. (NASB)

10. **When a child does come home and experiences God's renewed blessings, be prepared for people who do not understand** (or like) **grace and have adopted the "elder brother" attitude.**

    Luke 15:25–30 Now his older son was in the field, and as he came and drew near to the house, he heard music and dancing. And he called one of the servants and asked what these things meant. And he said to him, "Your brother has come, and your father has killed the fattened calf, because he has received him back safe and sound." But he was angry and refused to go in. His father came out and entreated him, but he answered his father, "Look, these many years I have served you, and I never disobeyed your command, yet you never gave me a young goat, that I might celebrate with my friends. But when this son of yours came, who has devoured your property with prostitutes, you killed the fattened calf for him!" (ESV)

Practical Steps

- Do your best to keep communication lines open. Anger, shouting, or kicking your child out will do nothing but destroy.
- Don't push for a quick resolution; be willing to wait as God does his work. Unwise pushing can stiffen your child's resistance.
- Seek wise counsel. Consider—are you majoring on externals or the heart of your child?
- Show consistent love—spend time with them; show affection by touching; send notes; use words that build up.

- Guard your walk and time with God so you are not brought down to discouragement, depression, defeat, or self-blame.

Resources

- *Hope and Help for Hurting Parents: When Good Kids Make Bad Choices*. Elyse Fitzpatrick. Harvest House.
- *Engaging Today's Prodigal: Clear Thinking, New Approaches, and Reasons for Hope*. Carol Barnier. Moody.
- *Parents with Broken Hearts*. William L. Coleman. BMH.
- *Prayers for Prodigals: 90 Days of Prayer for Your Child*. James Banks. Discovery House.
- *Prodigals and Those Who Love Them*. Ruth Graham. Baker.
- *When Your Kid's in Trouble* (booklet). William Smith. New Growth.

Health

See also **Aging, Disability, Grief, Trials, Trusting God**

1. **Health problems should elicit a response of love, support, renewed commitment, and sacrifice from one spouse to the other.**

   1 Corinthians 13:4–8 Love is patient and kind; love does not envy or boast; it is not arrogant or rude. It does not insist on its own way; it is not irritable or resentful; it does not rejoice at wrongdoing, but rejoices with the truth. Love bears all things, believes all things, hopes all things, endures all things. Love never ends. (ESV)

   Philippians 2:3–7 Rather, in humility value others above yourselves, not looking to your own interests but each of you to the interests of the others. In your relationships with one another, have the same mindset as Christ Jesus: Who, being in very nature God, did not consider equality with God something to be used to his own advantage; rather, he made himself nothing by taking the very nature of a servant. (NIV)

   Galatians 6:2 Bear one another's burdens, and so fulfill the law of Christ. (ESV)

   Ephesians 5:28–29 In this same way, husbands ought to love their wives as their own bodies. He who loves his wife loves himself. After all, no one ever hated their own body, but they feed and care for their body, just as Christ does the church. (NIV) (By application, the reverse would certainly be true in a wife's care for her husband.)

2. **Advice for healthy living from Proverbs:**

   Proverbs 3:7–8 Don't be impressed with your own wisdom. Instead, fear the LORD and turn away from evil. Then you will have healing for your body and strength for your bones. (NLT)

Proverbs 14:30 A peaceful heart leads to a healthy body; jealousy is like cancer in the bones. (NLT)

Proverbs 18:14 The human spirit can endure a sick body, but who can bear a crushed spirit? (NLT)

Proverbs 17:22 A cheerful heart is good medicine, but a broken spirit saps a person's strength. (NLT)

3. **God's presence in all trying situations is guaranteed. We are not alone.**

Joshua 1:9 This is my command—be strong and courageous! Do not be afraid or discouraged. For the LORD your God is with you wherever you go. (NLT)

Isaiah 43:1–2 But now, this is what the LORD says—he who created you, Jacob, he who formed you, Israel: "Do not fear, for I have redeemed you; I have summoned you by name; you are mine. When you pass through the waters, I will be with you; and when you pass through the rivers, they will not sweep over you. When you walk through the fire, you will not be burned; the flames will not set you ablaze." (NIV)

Isaiah 41:10, 13 So do not fear, for I am with you; do not be dismayed, for I am your God. I will strengthen you and help you; I will uphold you with my righteous right hand. . . . For I am the LORD your God who takes hold of your right hand and says to you, Do not fear; I will help you. (NIV)

Deuteronomy 31:6

4. **God gives strength to the weak.**

2 Samuel 22:33 This God is my strong refuge and has made my way blameless. (ESV)

Psalm 31:24 Be strong, and let your heart take courage, all you who wait for the LORD! (ESV)

Psalm 73:26 My flesh and my heart may fail, but God is the strength of my heart and my portion forever. (ESV)

Psalm 91:4 He will cover you with his pinions, and under his wings you will find refuge; his faithfulness is a shield and buckler. (ESV)

2 Corinthians 4:7–9 But we have this treasure in jars of clay, to show that the surpassing power belongs to God and not to us. We are afflicted in every way, but not crushed; perplexed, but not driven to despair; persecuted, but not forsaken; struck down, but not destroyed. (ESV)

Isaiah 40:30–31; 2 Corinthians 4:16

5. **God can and does heal, in his time, according to his will. God is the one who does the healing.**

Psalm 30:2–3 Lord my God, I called to you for help, and you healed me. You, Lord, brought me up from the realm of the dead; you spared me from going down to the pit. (NIV)

James 5:14–16 Is anyone among you sick? Let them call the elders of the church to pray over them and anoint them with oil in the name of the Lord. And the prayer offered in faith will make the sick person well; the Lord will raise them up. If they have sinned, they will be forgiven. Therefore confess your sins to each other and pray for each other so that you may be healed. The prayer of a righteous person is powerful and effective. (NIV)

2 Kings 20:1–11; Psalm 103:2–5

6. **Whatever the outcome of our health problems, God will be glorified.**

2 Corinthians 12:9–10 Each time he said, "My grace is all you need. My power works best in weakness." So now I am glad to boast about my weaknesses, so that the power of Christ can work through me. That's why I take pleasure in my weaknesses, and in the insults, hardships, persecutions, and troubles that I suffer for Christ. For when I am weak, then I am strong. (NLT)

1 Peter 1:6–7 So be truly glad. There is wonderful joy ahead, even though you must endure many trials for a little while. These trials will show that your faith is genuine. It is being tested as fire tests and purifies gold—though your faith is far more precious than mere gold. So when your faith remains strong through many trials, it will bring you much praise and glory and honor on the day when Jesus Christ is revealed to the whole world. (NLT)

Practical Steps

- Commit to regular exercise (if physically possible) and hold each other accountable. Whenever feasible, run, walk, or bike together. Help each other with physical therapy.
- Keep all your records and progress reports. Obtain copies of all tests. Do research; educate yourself so you are knowledgeable about treatments, risks, natural alternatives, and nutrition.
- Memorize Psalm 145:14–16. Review often.
- Post verses around your home that remind you of God's care. Read them often.
- If confined to home or bed, write and encourage others. Memorize Scripture; pray for missions; invite visitors.
- Have others pray with you and for you. Prayer is our lifeline!

Resources

- *Chronic Pain: Living by Faith When Your Body Hurts* (booklet). Michael Emlet. CCEF.
- *Making Sense of Suffering* (pamphlet). Joni Eareckson Tada. Rose.
- *Pain: The Plight of Fallen Man*. James Halla. Timeless Texts.
- *The Problem of Pain*. C. S. Lewis. Macmillan.

Disability

See also **Aging, Anxiety, Depression, Health**

1. **Caregiving responsibilities can become overwhelming.**

Psalm 69:1–3 Save me, O God, for the waters have come up to my neck. I sink in the miry depths, where there is no foothold. I have come into the deep waters; the floods engulf me. I am worn out calling for help; my throat is parched. My eyes fail, looking for my God. (NIV)

Psalm 6:4–6 Turn, LORD, and deliver me; save me because of your unfailing love. Among the dead no one proclaims your name. Who praises you from the grave? I am worn out from my groaning. All night long I flood my bed with weeping and drench my couch with tears. (NIV)

2. **God understands and encourages us in our weariness.**

Jeremiah 31:25 I will refresh the weary and satisfy the faint. (NIV)

Isaiah 40:28–31 Do you not know? Have you not heard? The LORD is the everlasting God, the Creator of the ends of the earth. He will not grow tired or weary, and his understanding no one can fathom. He gives strength to the weary and increases the power of the weak. Even youths grow tired and weary, and young men stumble and fall; but those who hope in the LORD will renew their strength. They will soar on wings like eagles; they will run and not grow weary, they will walk and not be faint. (NIV)

2 Thessalonians 3:13 And as for you, brothers and sisters, never tire of doing what is good. (NIV)

Hebrews 12:1–2 Let us run with determination the race that lies before us. Let us keep our eyes fixed on Jesus, on whom our faith depends from beginning to end. (GNT)

3. **Only death removes us from our responsibility for caring for our spouse.**

   Romans 7:2 For a married woman is bound by law to her husband while he lives, but if her husband dies she is released from the law of marriage. (ESV) (The context is divorce, but the principle applies here.)

   1 Timothy 5:8

4. **Note God's interest in caregiving.**

   Isaiah 46:4 Even to your old age and gray hairs I am he, I am he who will sustain you. I have made you and I will carry you; I will sustain you and I will rescue you. (NIV)

   Deuteronomy 1:30–31 The Lord your God, who is going before you, will fight for you, as he did for you in Egypt, before your very eyes, and in the wilderness. There you saw how the Lord your God carried you, as a father carries his son, all the way you went until you reached this place. (NIV) (The context here is Israel on the way to Canaan.)

5. **David's prayer in his old age for God's continued presence can apply to husbands and wives in their care for each other.**

   Psalm 71:17–18 Since my youth, God, you have taught me, and to this day I declare your marvelous deeds. Even when I am old and gray, do not forsake me, my God, till I declare your power to the next generation, your mighty acts to all who are to come. (NIV)

Practical Steps

- Proper care does not mean that you must do it all yourself. Others in your family or church will/should step up to assist.
- Always be mindful of your vows to each other—"in sickness and in health, 'til death us do part."
- Talk about the good times, the good memories when health was better. Get out the pictures, the videos. Thank God for the blessings that produced those memories.

- Together quote Scripture, sing hymns, play recordings.
- Ask God for strength, patience, and wisdom to offer quality care.
- Pray with the one you are caring for, especially regarding the details of the illness that generate anxiety.
- As the caregiver, take care of yourself. Find ways to get away, to take a break and renew.

Resources

- *Help for the Caregiver* (booklet). Michael Emlet. CCEF.
- "Hope for Caregivers of the Elderly" in *Women Counseling Women*. Elyse Fitzpatrick. Harvest House.
- *Help! Someone I Love Has Alzheimer's*. Deborah Howard. Day One.
- *Help! Someone I Love Has Cancer*. Deborah Howard. Day One.
- *When Is It Right to Die?* (booklet). Joni Eareckson Tada. Rose.

Trials

See also **Anger, Anxiety, Depression, Disappointment, Trusting God**

Job, in his great suffering, reminds us, "For man is born for trouble, as sparks fly upward" (5:7 NASB). No marriage, however blessed, is exempt from times of trial. Difficulties can separate; they can also bring us closer together. Certainly, for the couple whose anchor is Christ and his Word, confidently navigating deep water can be a reality.

Difficult Times Are a Part of Life

1. **We live in a fallen world where tough times are certain.**

   Genesis 3:17–19 And to Adam he said, "Because you have listened to the voice of your wife and have eaten of the tree of which I commanded you, 'You shall not eat of it,' cursed is the ground because of you; in pain you shall eat of it all the days of your life; thorns and thistles it shall bring forth for you; and you shall eat the plants of the field. By the sweat of your face you shall eat bread, till you return to the ground, for out of it you were taken; for you are dust, and to dust you shall return." (ESV)

   John 16:33 These things I have spoken to you, so that in Me you may have peace. In the world you have tribulation, but take courage; I have overcome the world. (NASB)

   Job 14:1–2; John 15:18–21; Romans 8:18–23

2. **Trials are to be expected and remind us of the sufferings of Christ.**

   1 Peter 4:12–13 Dear friends, don't be surprised at the fiery trials you are going through, as if something strange were happening to you. Instead, be very glad—for these trials make you partners with Christ in his suffering, so that you will have the wonderful joy of seeing his glory when it is revealed to all the world. (NLT)

2 Timothy 2:3 Take your part in suffering, as a loyal soldier of Christ Jesus. (GNT)

Why God Allows Trials

1. **God will use our experience with trials so we can help others.**

   2 Corinthians 1:3–5 All praise to God, the Father of our Lord Jesus Christ. God is our merciful Father and the source of all comfort. He comforts us in all our troubles so that we can comfort others. When they are troubled, we will be able to give them the same comfort God has given us. For the more we suffer for Christ, the more God will shower us with his comfort through Christ. (NLT)

2. **Our faith will be strengthened.**

   1 Peter 1:6–7 In all this you greatly rejoice, though now for a little while you may have had to suffer grief in all kinds of trials. These have come so that the proven genuineness of your faith—of greater worth than gold, which perishes even though refined by fire—may result in praise, glory and honor when Jesus Christ is revealed. (NIV)

   James 1:2–5 Consider it all joy, my brethren, when you encounter various trials, knowing that the testing of your faith produces endurance. And let endurance have its perfect result, so that you may be perfect and complete, lacking in nothing. But if any of you lacks wisdom, let him ask of God, who gives to all generously and without reproach, and it will be given to him. (NASB)

3. **Trials enable us to develop into the person God wants us to be.**

   Job 23:8–10 Behold, I go forward, but he is not there, and backward, but I do not perceive him; on the left hand when he is working, I do not behold him; he turns to the right hand, but

I do not see him. But he knows the way that I take; when he has tried me, I shall come out as gold. (ESV)

4. **Through trials we are driven to focus more on heaven and eternity.**

   2 Corinthians 4:17–18 And this small and temporary trouble we suffer will bring us a tremendous and eternal glory, much greater than the trouble. For we fix our attention, not on things that are seen, but on things that are unseen. What can be seen lasts only for a time, but what cannot be seen lasts forever. (GNT)

5. **A possible reason for trials is God's discipline that moves us to repentance and confession of sin.**

   Hebrews 12:10–11 For our earthly fathers disciplined us for a few years, doing the best they knew how. But God's discipline is always good for us, so that we might share in his holiness. No discipline is enjoyable while it is happening—it's painful! But afterward there will be a peaceful harvest of right living for those who are trained in this way. (NLT)

How We Must Respond

1. **Depending on God's presence and strength is crucial.**

   Psalm 3:4–5 I cried aloud to the LORD, and he answered me from his holy hill. I lay down and slept; I woke again, for the LORD sustained me. (ESV)

   Psalm 9:9–10 The LORD is a stronghold for the oppressed, a stronghold in times of trouble. And those who know your name put their trust in you, for you, O LORD, have not forsaken those who seek you. (ESV)

   Psalm 31:9–10 Be gracious to me, O LORD, for I am in distress; my eye is wasted from grief; my soul and my body also. For my life is spent with sorrow, and my years with sighing; my strength fails because of my iniquity, and my bones waste away. (ESV)

   Psalm 61:2 From the end of the earth I call to you when my heart is faint. Lead me to the rock that is higher than I. (ESV)

Psalm 86:3 Be gracious to me, O Lord, for to you do I cry all the day. (ESV)

2. **We can trust his sovereign wisdom and loving presence.**

   Jeremiah 10:23 LORD, I know that none of us are in charge of our own destiny; none of us have control over our own life. (GNT)

   Psalm 71:20–21 You have allowed me to suffer much hardship, but you will restore me to life again and lift me up from the depths of the earth. You will restore me to even greater honor and comfort me once again. (NLT)

   Isaiah 43:1–2 But now, thus says the LORD, your Creator, O Jacob, and He who formed you, O Israel, "Do not fear, for I have redeemed you; I have called you by name; you are Mine! When you pass through the waters, I will be with you; and through the rivers, they will not overflow you. When you walk through the fire, you will not be scorched, nor will the flame burn you." (NASB)

   2 Timothy 4:17–18 But the Lord stayed with me and gave me strength, so that I was able to proclaim the full message for all the Gentiles to hear; and I was rescued from being sentenced to death. And the Lord will rescue me from all evil and take me safely into his heavenly Kingdom. To him be the glory forever and ever! Amen. (GNT)

   Psalm 23; 56:8; John 14:27; 2 Thessalonians 3:16

3. **Our need is the recognition of his sufficient grace.**

   Psalm 55:22 Cast your burden on the LORD, and he will sustain you; he will never permit the righteous to be moved. (ESV)

   2 Corinthians 12:9 But he said to me, "My grace is sufficient for you, for my power is made perfect in weakness." Therefore I will boast all the more gladly of my weaknesses, so that the power of Christ may rest upon me. (ESV)

4. **As we are strong through adversity, God's reward will be evident.**

   James 1:12 Blessed is the man who remains steadfast under trial, for when he has stood the test he will receive the crown of life, which God has promised to those who love him. (ESV)

Practical Steps

- Both of you need to keep a daily prayer journal, noting your pain and struggles. Record answers as God responds. Every day, list items of thanksgiving. Share with each other.
- Memorize Isaiah 43:1–2. Write it on a card and keep it close at hand.
- Be open with other believing couples. Enlist them to empathize with and pray for you.
- Seek out others going through trials; encourage them by listening to their stories and praying faithfully for them.
- Meditate on Romans 8:28 and write down a difficult event in your past that God has used for good.
- Center your Bible reading on the Psalms where the authors experienced adversity, such as 13, 34, 46, 55, 73, 91, 121, 143, and 145.

Resources

- *The Comeback: It's Not Too Late and You're Never Too Far*. Louie Giglio. Passion Publishing.
- *Making Sense of Suffering* (pamphlet). Joni Eareckson Tada. Rose.
- *Reaching for the Invisible God*. Philip Yancey. Zondervan.
- *Trusting God: Even When Life Hurts*. Jerry Bridges. NavPress.
- "The Wisdom of God" in *God: As He Longs for You to See Him*. Chip Ingram. Baker.

Death

See also **Anxiety, Grief, Trials, Trusting God**

No one has any guarantee that tomorrow will come. Death of immediate family members is the most feared event, and for many, death of a child or spouse is the worst. Paul refers to death as the "last enemy to be destroyed" (1 Cor. 15:26 ESV). From a purely human standpoint, death is the great plague from which no human is exempt. But through Christ, redemption and resurrection are guaranteed.

Death as a Reality

1. **Death comes to every human being. Sad to say, but gravity wins in the end.**

   Genesis 3:19 By the sweat of your brow you will eat your food until you return to the ground, since from it you were taken; for dust you are and to dust you will return. (NIV)

   Psalm 90:10 Our days may come to seventy years, or eighty, if our strength endures; yet the best of them are but trouble and sorrow, for they quickly pass, and we fly away. (NIV)

   Hebrews 9:27 Each person is destined to die once and after that comes judgment. (NLT)

   Ecclesiastes 3:1–4

2. **Death is in God's sovereign hands. The timing is totally his.**

   Psalm 39:4–5 Lord, remind me how brief my time on earth will be. Remind me that my days are numbered—how fleeting my life is. You have made my life no longer than the width of my hand. My entire lifetime is just a moment to you; at best, each of us is but a breath. (NLT)

Psalm 90:5–6 Yet you sweep people away in the sleep of death—they are like the new grass of the morning: In the morning it springs up new, but by evening it is dry and withered. (NIV)

Matthew 10:29–31

Facing Death with Hope

1. **Not even death can separate us from God and his love.**

   Psalm 23:4 Even though I walk through the valley of the shadow of death, I will fear no evil, for you are with me; your rod and your staff, they comfort me. (ESV)

   Psalm 116:15 Precious in the sight of the Lord is the death of his saints. (ESV)

   Romans 8:38–39 For I am sure that neither death nor life, nor angels nor rulers, nor things present nor things to come, nor powers, nor height nor depth, nor anything else in all creation, will be able to separate us from the love of God in Christ Jesus our Lord. (ESV)

   Joshua 1:9; Psalm 73:26

2. **Death for the believer means being in the presence of Christ.**

   Philippians 1:21–23 For to me to live is Christ, and to die is gain. If I am to live in the flesh, that means fruitful labor for me. Yet which I shall choose I cannot tell. I am hard pressed between the two. My desire is to depart and be with Christ, for that is far better. (ESV)

   2 Corinthians 5:6–8 So we are always confident, even though we know that as long as we live in these bodies we are not at home with the Lord. For we live by believing and not by seeing. Yes, we are fully confident, and we would rather be away from these earthly bodies, for then we will be at home with the Lord. (NLT)

   Job 19:25–26; Psalm 49:15; Isaiah 57:2; John 14:1–3

3. **Death for the believer means receiving a changed and glorified body.**

John 11:25–26 Jesus told her, "I am the resurrection and the life. Anyone who believes in me will live, even after dying. Everyone who lives in me and believes in me will never ever die. Do you believe this, Martha?" (NLT)

Philippians 3:21 He will take our weak mortal bodies and change them into glorious bodies like his own, using the same power with which he will bring everything under his control. (NLT)

1 Corinthians 15:51–53 But let me reveal to you a wonderful secret. We will not all die, but we will all be transformed! It will happen in a moment, in the blink of an eye, when the last trumpet is blown. For when the trumpet sounds, those who have died will be raised to live forever. And we who are living will also be transformed. For our dying bodies must be transformed into bodies that will never die; our mortal bodies must be transformed into immortal bodies. (NLT)

John 6:40; 1 John 3:2

4. **Jesus's death and resurrection provide ultimate freedom from fear of death, in heaven.**

1 Peter 1:3–5 Blessed be the God and Father of our Lord Jesus Christ! According to his great mercy, he has caused us to be born again to a living hope through the resurrection of Jesus Christ from the dead, to an inheritance that is imperishable, undefiled, and unfading, kept in heaven for you, who by God's power are being guarded through faith for a salvation ready to be revealed in the last time. (ESV)

Revelation 21:3–4 And I heard a loud voice from the throne saying, "Behold, the dwelling place of God is with man. He will dwell with them, and they will be his people, and God himself will be with them as their God. He will wipe away every tear from their eyes, and death shall be no more, neither shall there be mourning, nor crying, nor pain anymore, for the former things have passed away." (ESV)

1 Corinthians 15:20–26; Hebrews 2:9–15

5. **Hold on to these comforting words from Isaiah:**

   Isaiah 25:8–9 He will swallow up death forever; and the Lord God will wipe away tears from all faces, and the reproach of his people he will take away from all the earth, for the Lord has spoken. It will be said on that day, "Behold, this is our God; we have waited for him, that he might save us. This is the Lord; we have waited for him; let us be glad and rejoice in his salvation." (ESV)

   Isaiah 41:10, 13 Fear not, for I am with you; be not dismayed, for I am your God; I will strengthen you, I will help you, I will uphold you with my righteous right hand. . . . For I, the Lord your God, hold your right hand; it is I who say to you, "Fear not, I am the one who helps you." (ESV)

   Isaiah 58:11 And the Lord will guide you continually and satisfy your desire in scorched places and make your bones strong; and you shall be like a watered garden, like a spring of water, whose waters do not fail. (ESV)

   Isaiah 51:11–12 So the ransomed of the Lord will return and come with joyful shouting to Zion, and everlasting joy will be on their heads. They will obtain gladness and joy, and sorrow and sighing will flee away. I, even I, am He who comforts you. (NASB)

6. **God understands and has compassion for our broken hearts. He can use our loss to bring us closer to himself.**

   Psalm 34:18 The Lord is near to the brokenhearted and saves the crushed in spirit. (ESV)

   Psalm 147:3 He heals the brokenhearted and binds up their wounds. (ESV)

   Matthew 5:4 Blessed are those who mourn, for they shall be comforted. (ESV)

   John 14:27 Peace I leave with you; my peace I give to you. Not as the world gives do I give to you. Let not your hearts be troubled, neither let them be afraid. (ESV)

   John 14:1

7. **Death for the unbeliever results in the separation, darkness, and pain of hell. (See topic "The Gospel.")**

   Matthew 22:13; 2 Thessalonians 1:7–9; Revelation 20:11–15

Practical Steps

- If it is your spouse who has died, make sure you get out and do things with others, especially other strong believers. Don't stay at home, alone with your grief.
- Psalms to read when you feel fear of death—23, 31, 34, 46, 91. Copy specific verses on cards and keep them close at hand.
- Memorize Revelation 21:3–4.
- Make sure your time alone with God is consistent every day (Scripture and prayer).
- Research and study the stages of grief.

Resources

- "After the Funeral" in *The Hand of God: Finding His Care in All Circumstances*. Alistair Begg. Moody
- *Facing Death with Hope* (booklet). David Powlison. New Growth.
- *Grief Undone: A Journey with God and Cancer*. Elizabeth W. D. Groves. New Growth.
- *One Minute After You Die*. Erwin Lutzer. Moody.
- *Questions Children and Adults Ask about Death* (booklet). Wally Stephenson. RBP.

Failure

See also **Depression, Disappointment, Grief, Trials, Trusting God**

1. **Central to success in life (and marriage) is knowing God personally through Christ. In the end, it's not about how smart we are or how much power or wealth we have. We live for an audience of One!**

   Jeremiah 9:23–24 Thus says the Lord: "Let not the wise man boast in his wisdom, let not the mighty man boast in his might, let not the rich man boast in his riches, but let him who boasts boast in this, that he understands and knows me, that I am the Lord who practices steadfast love, justice, and righteousness in the earth. For in these things I delight, declares the Lord." (ESV)

   Psalm 73:25–26 Whom have I in heaven but you? And there is nothing on earth that I desire besides you. My flesh and my heart may fail, but God is the strength of my heart and my portion forever. (ESV)

   Galatians 6:14 But far be it from me to boast except in the cross of our Lord Jesus Christ, by which the world has been crucified to me, and I to the world. (ESV)

2. **God's expectations for the success of his children include the following:**

   2 Chronicles 16:9 For the eyes of the Lord run to and fro throughout the whole earth, to give strong support to those whose heart is blameless toward him. (ESV)

   Micah 6:8 He has told you, O man, what is good; and what does the Lord require of you but to do justice, and to love kindness, and to walk humbly with your God? (ESV)

John 15:4–5 Abide in me, and I in you. As the branch cannot bear fruit by itself, unless it abides in the vine, neither can you, unless you abide in me. I am the vine; you are the branches. Whoever abides in me and I in him, he it is that bears much fruit, for apart from me you can do nothing. (ESV)

3. **Study of and obedience to God's Word is the path to success.**

Deuteronomy 32:46–47 Take to heart all the words by which I am warning you today, that you may command them to your children, that they may be careful to do all the words of this law. For it is no empty word for you, but your very life, and by this word you shall live long in the land that you are going over the Jordan to possess. (ESV)

Joshua 1:8–9 This Book of the Law shall not depart from your mouth, but you shall meditate on it day and night, so that you may be careful to do according to all that is written in it. For then you will make your way prosperous, and then you will have good success. Have I not commanded you? Be strong and courageous. Do not be frightened, and do not be dismayed, for the LORD your God is with you wherever you go. (ESV)

Jeremiah 6:16; Hebrews 4:12

4. **God must receive the credit for whatever success we enjoy.**

1 Corinthians 3:6–9 I planted the seed, Apollos watered it, but God has been making it grow. So neither the one who plants nor the one who waters is anything, but only God, who makes things grow. The one who plants and the one who waters have one purpose, and they will each be rewarded according to their own labor. For we are co-workers in God's service; you are God's field, God's building. (NIV) (The context here is church growth, but the principle applies.)

1 Corinthians 15:10 By the grace of God I am what I am, and his grace to me was not without effect. No, I worked harder than all of them—yet not I, but the grace of God that was with me. (NIV)

James 4:13–15 Now listen, you who say, "Today or tomorrow we will go to this or that city, spend a year there, carry on business and make money." Why, you do not even know what will happen tomorrow. What is your life? You are a mist that appears for a little while and then vanishes. Instead, you ought to say, "If it is the Lord's will, we will live and do this or that." (NIV)

5. **Though we sometimes fail, God will never fail us. Our trust needs to be strong in him.**

Habakkuk 3:17–19 Though the fig tree should not blossom, nor fruit be on the vines, the produce of the olive fail and the fields yield no food, the flock be cut off from the fold and there be no herd in the stalls, yet I will rejoice in the Lord; I will take joy in the God of my salvation. God, the Lord, is my strength; he makes my feet like the deer's; he makes me tread on my high places. (ESV)

Psalm 145:14–19 The Lord upholds all who fall and lifts up all who are bowed down. The eyes of all look to you, and you give them their food at the proper time. You open your hand and satisfy the desires of every living thing. The Lord is righteous in all his ways and faithful in all he does. The Lord is near to all who call on him, to all who call on him in truth. He fulfills the desires of those who fear him; he hears their cry and saves them. (NIV)

Isaiah 58:11 And the Lord will guide you continually and satisfy your desire in scorched places and make your bones strong; and you shall be like a watered garden, like a spring of water, whose waters do not fail. (ESV) (The context here is helping others.)

Deuteronomy 31:6–8; Joshua 21:45; Psalm 34:4–7; Lamentations 3:21–24; Matthew 7:7–11

6. **Our weakness is God's strength.**

Isaiah 40:28–31 Have you not known? Have you not heard? The Lord is the everlasting God, the Creator of the ends of the earth. He does not faint or grow weary; his understanding is unsearchable. He gives power to the faint, and to him who has no might he increases strength. Even youths shall faint and be weary, and young men shall fall exhausted; but they who wait for the LORD shall renew their strength; they shall mount up with wings like eagles; they shall run and not be weary; they shall walk and not faint. (ESV)

2 Corinthians 12:9–10

7. **When we experience failure, God wants us to not give up, and to find new ways to succeed.**

1 Corinthians 9:24–25 Do you not know that in a race all the runners run, but only one gets the prize? Run in such a way as to get the prize. Everyone who competes in the games goes into strict training. They do it to get a crown that will not last, but we do it to get a crown that will last forever. (NIV)

Philippians 3:12–14 I do not claim that I have already succeeded or have already become perfect. I keep striving to win the prize for which Christ Jesus has already won me to himself. Of course, my friends, I really do not think that I have already won it; the one thing I do, however, is to forget what is behind me and do my best to reach what is ahead. So I run straight toward the goal in order to win the prize, which is God's call through Christ Jesus to the life above. (GNT)

2 Timothy 1:6–7 For this reason I remind you to keep alive the gift that God gave you when I laid my hands on you. For the Spirit that God has given us does not make us timid; instead, his Spirit fills us with power, love, and self-control. (GNT)

8. **If our failure involves personal sin, repentance and confession are necessary to get our lives back on track. (See topics "Confession" and "Forgiveness from God.")**

9. **Consider the example of these Bible characters who struggled.**

David sinned but was forgiven.

2 Samuel 11–12; Psalm 51

Peter denied the Lord but was restored to service.
John 18:15–27; 21:15–19; Acts 2

John Mark was unfaithful but received another chance.
Acts 15:36–40; 2 Timothy 4:11

Timothy was burned out and in need of rekindling.
2 Timothy 1–2

Paul pressed on in spite of his past.
Philippians 3:8–14

Practical Steps

- If it is your spouse who has experienced failure, make sure you are understanding and supportive and not bitter, blaming, or unforgiving.
- Make sure your lives are centered on God's definition of success (#1 above). Contrast that with the world's view. Study 1 John 2:15–17 to understand what to avoid.
- Don't dwell on the past. Focus on blessings from God and what he will do in the future.
- Study and memorize Philippians 3:13–14 and 4:8; copy the verses on a card and keep it close as a reminder.
- Share concerns with other men and women who are mature in Christ. Open your heart to them. Get them praying for you and holding you accountable.

Resources

- *Can God Be Trusted in Our Trials?* Tony Evans. Moody.
- *The Comeback: It's Not Too Late and You're Never Too Far.* Louie Giglio. Passion Publishing.

- *Failure: The Back Door to Success*. Erwin Lutzer. Moody.
- *Finding God When You Need Him Most*. Chip Ingram. Baker.
- *A Shelter in the Time of Storm*. Paul Tripp. Crossway.

Job Loss

See also **Anxiety, Decision Making, Depression, Disappointment, Trusting God**

You didn't see it coming (or maybe you did), but suddenly you are in the ranks of the unemployed. Immediate feelings might include sorrow, fear, anger, bitterness, regret. How do you tell your spouse, or your children? What will this mean to them? What do you do now? Where do you turn? Believers have hope in a God who is sovereign.

1. **God promises the security of his presence—no matter what.**

   Joshua 1:9 Have I not commanded you? Be strong and courageous. Do not be frightened, and do not be dismayed, for the Lord your God is with you wherever you go. (ESV)

   Deuteronomy 31:8 It is the Lord who goes before you. He will be with you; he will not leave you or forsake you. Do not fear or be dismayed. (ESV)

   Psalm 9:10 And those who know your name put their trust in you, for you, O Lord, have not forsaken those who seek you. (ESV)

   Hebrews 13:5–6 Keep your life free from love of money, and be content with what you have, for he has said, "I will never leave you nor forsake you." So we can confidently say, "The Lord is my helper; I will not fear; what can man do to me?" (ESV)

2. **God promises to guide us and provide for our needs—no matter what.**

   Psalm 32:8 I will instruct you and teach you in the way you should go; I will counsel you with my eye upon you. (ESV)

   Psalm 143:8 Let me hear in the morning of your steadfast love, for in you I trust. Make me know the way I should go, for to you I lift up my soul. (ESV)

1 Chronicles 29:11–13 Yours, O Lord, is the greatness and the power and the glory and the victory and the majesty, for all that is in the heavens and in the earth is yours. Yours is the kingdom, O Lord, and you are exalted as head above all. Both riches and honor come from you, and you rule over all. In your hand are power and might, and in your hand it is to make great and to give strength to all. And now we thank you, our God, and praise your glorious name. (ESV)

Philippians 4:19 And my God will supply every need of yours according to his riches in glory in Christ Jesus. (ESV)

Proverbs 3:5–6; Psalm 37:23–25; 50:12; Haggai 2:8

3. **God can replace our fear with confidence.**

Psalm 56:2–4 My foes have trampled upon me all day long, for they are many who fight proudly against me. When I am afraid, I will put my trust in You. In God, whose word I praise, in God I have put my trust; I shall not be afraid. What can mere man do to me? (NASB)

Psalm 71:5

4. **God's compassion for our loss is a reality.**

Psalm 103:13 As a father shows compassion to his children, so the Lord shows compassion to those who fear him. (ESV)

Isaiah 54:10 "For the mountains may depart and the hills be removed, but my steadfast love shall not depart from you, and my covenant of peace shall not be removed," says the Lord, who has compassion on you. (ESV)

Lamentations 3:19–24

Our God is:

Our rock

2 Samuel 22:2–4 The Lord is my rock and my fortress and my deliverer, my God, my rock, in whom I take refuge, my shield, and the horn of my salvation, my stronghold and my refuge, my savior; you save me from violence. I call upon the LORD, who is worthy to be praised, and I am saved from my enemies. (ESV)

Isaiah 26:4 Trust in the LORD forever, for the LORD GOD is an everlasting rock. (ESV)

Psalm 18:2; 19:14

Our refuge

Psalm 46:1–3 God is our refuge and strength, a very present help in trouble. Therefore we will not fear though the earth gives way, though the mountains be moved into the heart of the sea, though its waters roar and foam, though the mountains tremble at its swelling. (ESV)

Hebrews 6:18–20 So that by two unchangeable things, in which it is impossible for God to lie, we who have fled for refuge might have strong encouragement to hold fast to the hope set before us. We have this as a sure and steadfast anchor of the soul, a hope that enters into the inner place behind the curtain, where Jesus has gone as a forerunner on our behalf, having become a high priest forever after the order of Melchizedek. (ESV)

Our strength

Psalm 28:7–8 The LORD is my strength and my shield; in him my heart trusts, and I am helped; my heart exults, and with my song I give thanks to him. The LORD is the strength of his people; he is the saving refuge of his anointed. (ESV)

Our stronghold

Psalm 37:39–40 The salvation of the righteous is from the LORD; he is their stronghold in the time of trouble. The LORD helps them and delivers them; he delivers them from the wicked and saves them, because they take refuge in him. (ESV)

Practical Steps

- Cutting back your expenses is most likely necessary. Check out the Dave Ramsey books, recordings, and website for help.
- Use your time off to build deeper relationships with your husband or wife and children. If financially able, do those special things you've wanted to do but time did not allow.
- Communicate your concerns to your spouse and other strong Christians. Be open and straightforward—don't internalize your feelings.
- Whatever the reason for your job loss, work on not being bitter or vengeful, forgiving those involved if needed.
- Evaluate. Are there areas in which you can grow, improve, or learn? Be willing and teachable.

Resources

- "The Faithfulness of God" in *God: As He Longs for You to See Him*. Chip Ingram. Baker.
- *God Cannot Be Trusted (and Five Other Lies of Satan)*. Tony Evans. Moody.
- "Replacing a Doubtful Heart . . . with an Attitude of Trust" in *Lord, Change My Attitude*. James McDonald and Erwin Lutzer. Moody.
- *Trusting God: Even When Life Hurts*. Jerry Bridges. NavPress.

Divorce

See also **Abuse, Anger, Anxiety, Grief, Self-Worth, Trials**

This was never on your radar; divorce was not on your mind when you got married. Yet the sad reality in our broken world is that it does happen, even to Christians. This topic is controversial, especially the question of remarriage. Bible scholars have different conclusions. No matter what the issues in the marriage, the goal must first and foremost be to seek reconciliation, saving the marriage. Divorce is a last resort.

1. **Faithful commitment to your spouse is commanded by God.**

   Malachi 2:14 You cry out, "Why doesn't the Lord accept my worship?" I'll tell you why! Because the Lord witnessed the vows you and your wife made when you were young. But you have been unfaithful to her, though she remained your faithful partner, the wife of your marriage vows. (NLT) (The application is also to the wife.)

   Matthew 5:27–28 You have heard the commandment that says, "You must not commit adultery." But I say, anyone who even looks at a woman with lust has already committed adultery with her in his heart. (NLT)

2. **God's plan is for marriage to be permanent.**

   Malachi 2:15–16 So guard your heart; remain loyal to the wife of your youth. "For I hate divorce!" says the Lord, the God of Israel. "To divorce your wife is to overwhelm her with cruelty," says the Lord of Heaven's Armies. "So guard your heart; do not be unfaithful to your wife." (NLT)

   Matthew 19:6 So they are no longer two, but one flesh. What therefore God has joined together, let no man separate. (NASB)

   Genesis 2:22–25; Mark 10:3–5

3. Marriage difficulties are not insurmountable. Incompatibility can be improved and should not be a valid reason for divorce.

1 Corinthians 13:4–7 Love is patient and kind. Love is not jealous or boastful or proud or rude. It does not demand its own way. It is not irritable, and it keeps no record of being wronged. It does not rejoice about injustice but rejoices whenever the truth wins out. Love never gives up, never loses faith, is always hopeful, and endures through every circumstance. (NLT)

Philippians 2:1–8 Is there any encouragement from belonging to Christ? Any comfort from his love? Any fellowship together in the Spirit? Are your hearts tender and compassionate? Then make me truly happy by agreeing wholeheartedly with each other, loving one another, and working together with one mind and purpose. Don't be selfish; don't try to impress others. Be humble, thinking of others as better than yourselves. Don't look out only for your own interests, but take an interest in others, too. You must have the same attitude that Christ Jesus had. Though he was God, he did not think of equality with God as something to cling to. Instead, he gave up his divine privileges; he took the humble position of a slave and was born as a human being. (NLT)

1 Peter 3:7 In the same way, you husbands must give honor to your wives. Treat your wife with understanding as you live together. She may be weaker than you are, but she is your equal partner in God's gift of new life. Treat her as you should so your prayers will not be hindered. (NLT)

Philippians 4:8, 13

4. A spouse who is an unbeliever is not a reason for divorce.

1 Corinthians 7:12–13 But to the rest I say, not the Lord, that if any brother has a wife who is an unbeliever, and she consents to live with him, he must not divorce her. And a woman who has an unbelieving husband, and he consents to live with her, she must not send her husband away. (NASB)

5. **Whatever the problems in a marriage, reconciliation and restoration are always the goals and the best option.**

   1 Corinthians 7:10–11 To the married I give this command (not I, but the Lord): A wife must not separate from her husband. But if she does, she must remain unmarried or else be reconciled to her husband. And a husband must not divorce his wife. (NIV)

   Galatians 6:1–2 Brethren, even if anyone is caught in any trespass, you who are spiritual, restore such a one in a spirit of gentleness; each one looking to yourself, so that you too will not be tempted. Bear one another's burdens, and thereby fulfill the law of Christ. (NASB)

   Hebrews 12:14–15 Make every effort to live in peace with everyone and to be holy; without holiness no one will see the Lord. See to it that no one falls short of the grace of God and that no bitter root grows up to cause trouble and defile many. (NIV)

6. **God allows divorce when there has been unfaithfulness and/or desertion by an unbelieving spouse. However, seeking reconciliation should be the goal.**

   Matthew 5:31–32 It has been said, "Anyone who divorces his wife must give her a certificate of divorce." But I tell you that anyone who divorces his wife, except for sexual immorality, makes her the victim of adultery, and anyone who marries a divorced woman commits adultery. (NIV)

   1 Corinthians 7:15 But if the unbeliever leaves, let it be so. The brother or the sister is not bound in such circumstances; God has called us to live in peace. (NIV)

7. **If divorce does happen, remarriage after divorce is biblically acceptable in three situations.**

   If the divorce took place before becoming a believer

   2 Corinthians 5:17 Therefore, if anyone is in Christ, he is a new creation; old things have passed away; behold, all things have become new. (NKJV)

If the divorce happened because of the unrepentant unfaithfulness of the spouse

Matthew 19:9 I tell you that anyone who divorces his wife, except for sexual immorality, and marries another woman commits adultery. (NIV)

If an unbelieving spouse deserts a believing spouse

1 Corinthians 7:15 But if the unbeliever leaves, let it be so. The brother or the sister is not bound in such circumstances; God has called us to live in peace. (NIV)

Practical Steps

- See topic "Abuse" if that is a part of your situation.
- Commit before you marry that divorce will never be an option.
- Make sure you are seeking your spouse's greatest good, living sacrificially for him or her, renewing your covenant often.
- Research the top reasons why people divorce. Construct a plan to prevent these in your marriage.
- If you are sinning, repent! Make a renewed commitment to live in obedience to God.
- If your spouse is sinning, make sure you do not fall into the trap of anger, bitterness, ungodly living, gossip, lack of self-control, or hurtful speech. Whatever is happening, do not permit it to cause you to choose sin.
- Seek intensive biblical counseling to reconcile and restore your marriage.

Resources

- *Divorce* (booklet). Charles Swindoll. Multnomah. (grace view)
- *The Divorce Dilemma*. John MacArthur. Day One. (grace view)
- *The Divorce Myth*. J. Carl Laney. Bethany House. (restrictive view)

- "Separating What God Has Joined Together: Divorce and Remarriage" in *God, Marriage, and Family*. Andreas Kostenberger. Crossway.
- *Tying the Knot Tighter: Because Marriage Lasts a Lifetime*. Martha Peace and John Crotts. P&R.

Aging

See also **Contentment, Death, Priorities**

"Grow old with me—the best is yet to be." As God is willing, the two of you will grow old together. Yet, aging does have its setbacks. And in our youth-oriented society, aging is seen by many as something to avoid at all costs. The Bible addresses the inevitability of aging and provides positive encouragement. What about the "American dream," retirement? What should be the Christian's response? Is it a biblical concept at all?

1. **Wisdom comes from Solomon on life's brevity and its enjoyment. Notice the need to factor God into life's equation, making sure he is at the very center.**

   Ecclesiastes 5:18–19 Even so, I have noticed one thing, at least, that is good. It is good for people to eat, drink, and enjoy their work under the sun during the short life God has given them, and to accept their lot in life. And it is a good thing to receive wealth from God and the good health to enjoy it. To enjoy your work and accept your lot in life—this is indeed a gift from God. (NLT)

   Ecclesiastes 3:12–13 So I concluded there is nothing better than to be happy and enjoy ourselves as long as we can. And people should eat and drink and enjoy the fruits of their labor, for these are gifts from God. (NLT)

   Ecclesiastes 9:7–9 Go then, eat your bread in happiness and drink your wine with a cheerful heart; for God has already approved your works. Let your clothes be white all the time, and let not oil be lacking on your head. Enjoy life with the woman whom you love all the days of your fleeting life which He has

given to you under the sun; for this is your reward in life and in your toil in which you have labored under the sun. (NASB)
Ecclesiastes 2:24–25; 3:22

2. **Since our days are short, we need to give them all over to God, wisely trusting him for the days we have.**

James 4:14–15 You do not know what tomorrow will bring. What is your life? For you are a mist that appears for a little time and then vanishes. Instead you ought to say, "If the Lord wills, we will live and do this or that." (ESV)

Job 14:1–2, 5 How frail is humanity! How short is life, how full of trouble! We blossom like a flower and then wither. Like a passing shadow, we quickly disappear. . . . You have decided the length of our lives. You know how many months we will live, and we are not given a minute longer. (NLT)

Psalm 39:5–6 You have made my life no longer than the width of my hand. My entire lifetime is just a moment to you; at best, each of us is but a breath. We are merely moving shadows, and all our busy rushing ends in nothing. We heap up wealth, not knowing who will spend it. (NLT)

Psalm 90:3–4, 10 You return man to dust and say, "Return, O children of man!" For a thousand years in your sight are but as yesterday when it is past, or as a watch in the night. . . . The years of our life are seventy, or even by reason of strength eighty; yet their span is but toil and trouble; they are soon gone, and we fly away. (ESV)

3. **When God allows us to live to an advanced age, we must be thankful. It is a wonderful gift to be able to enjoy that time with the wife or husband of your youth.**

Proverbs 16:31 Gray hair is a crown of splendor; it is attained in the way of righteousness. (NIV)

Proverbs 20:29 The glory of young men is their strength, gray hair the splendor of the old. (NIV)

Psalm 118:24 This is the day that the Lord has made; let us rejoice and be glad in it. (ESV)

4. **The fact that the stages of life move by so quickly is a reminder to make the best of the years we are allowed, glorifying God each day.**

Psalm 90:12 So teach us to number our days that we may get a heart of wisdom. (ESV)

Psalm 115:1 Not to us, O LORD, not to us, but to your name give glory, for the sake of your steadfast love and your faithfulness! (ESV)

Psalm 34:12–15 What man is there who desires life and loves many days, that he may see good? Keep your tongue from evil and your lips from speaking deceit. Turn away from evil and do good; seek peace and pursue it. The eyes of the LORD are toward the righteous and his ears toward their cry. (ESV)

2 Corinthians 5:9 More than anything else, however, we want to please him, whether in our home here or there. (GNT)

Psalm 72:19; 79:9; 1 Corinthians 10:31

5. **The seasons of life are in God's hand, and he generously provides.**

Psalm 71:6–9 Yes, you have been with me from birth; from my mother's womb you have cared for me. No wonder I am always praising you! My life is an example to many, because you have been my strength and protection. That is why I can never stop praising you; I declare your glory all day long. And now, in my old age, don't set me aside. Don't abandon me when my strength is failing. (NLT)

Isaiah 46:4 Even to your old age and gray hairs I am he, I am he who will sustain you. I have made you and I will carry you; I will sustain you and I will rescue you. (NIV)

Isaiah 35:3–4 Strengthen the weak hands, and make firm the feeble knees. Say to those who have an anxious heart, "Be strong; fear not! Behold, your God will come with vengeance, with the recompense of God. He will come and save you." (ESV)

Isaiah 58:11 The LORD will guide you continually, and satisfy your soul in drought, and strengthen your bones; you shall be like a watered garden, and like a spring of water, whose waters do not fail. (NKJV)

Isaiah 40:27–31

6. **Our senior years should be a productive time. If retirement means slowing down and not working as much to make money, that is acceptable, but we should always be serving God and others through all of our days.**

    Job 12:12 Wisdom is with the aged, and understanding in length of days. (ESV)

    Psalm 71:18 So even to old age and gray hairs, O God, do not forsake me, until I proclaim your might to another generation, your power to all those to come. (ESV)

    Psalm 92:12–14 But the godly will flourish like palm trees and grow strong like the cedars of Lebanon. For they are transplanted to the Lord's own house. They flourish in the courts of our God. Even in old age they will still produce fruit; they will remain vital and green. (NLT)

    Galatians 6:9 And let us not grow weary of doing good, for in due season we will reap, if we do not give up. (ESV)

    1 Corinthians 15:58 Therefore, my beloved brothers, be steadfast, immovable, always abounding in the work of the Lord, knowing that in the Lord your labor is not in vain. (ESV)

    2 Thessalonians 3:13

7. **Caleb and Paul are models for maturing with a godly attitude.**

    Joshua 14:1–15; 2 Timothy 4:6–8

Practical Steps

- Memorize and meditate frequently on Ephesians 5:15–17.
- Exercise together as a couple frequently, if possible. "If you don't use it, you'll lose it," is very real.
- Choose activities that stimulate the brain—Sudoku, crossword puzzles, jigsaw puzzles—which are essentials for mental and emotional health as well.
- Keep actively ministering to others—visit a nursing home, be a hospital volunteer. Reach out—make calls and send letters. Invest in the lives of others.

- Invest in the lives of young people—children or teens. Be mentors for young couples.
- Make a timeline of important life events, thanking God for his care.
- Print out Isaiah 46:4 on a 3x5 card. Post it or carry it. Review often.
- Each morning read Psalm 71:18: "Even when I am old and gray, do not forsake me, my God, till I declare your power to the next generation, your mighty acts to all who are to come" (NIV).

Resources

- *Afternoon of Life*. Elyse Fitzpatrick. P&R.
- *The Art of Aging*. Howard Eyrich. Focus.
- *Lost in the Middle: Midlife and the Grace of God*. Paul Tripp. Shepherd.
- "Retirement" and "Aging" in *The Strength of a Man* (devotional). David Roper. Discovery House.
- *Sunsets: Reflections for Life's Final Journey*. Deborah Howard. Crossway.
- *Wrinkled but Not Ruined*. Jay Adams. Timeless Texts.

Empty Nest

See also **Aging, Anxiety, Depression, Grief, Parenting, Selfishness**

This metaphor is a beautiful expression from God's creative design in nature experienced by most birds and other nesting animals. Offspring come to maturity and leave home to go out on their own. That's the way it's supposed to work. On occasion, human parents struggle deeply with this reality, and pain or regret becomes a part of the experience. Consider the help Scripture can provide.

Understanding God's Plan

1. **The goal for Christian parents in raising children is to have them leave home as mature, God-honoring adults, grounded in Scripture, prepared to establish their own homes.**

   Genesis 2:24 For this reason a man shall leave his father and his mother, and be joined to his wife; and they shall become one flesh. (NASB)

   Proverbs 17:6 Grandchildren are the crowning glory of the aged; parents are the pride of their children. (NLT)

   Psalm 78:5–6 For he issued his laws to Jacob; he gave his instructions to Israel. He commanded our ancestors to teach them to their children, so the next generation might know them—even the children not yet born—and they in turn will teach their own children. (NLT)

   Joel 1:3 Tell your children about it in the years to come, and let your children tell their children. Pass the story down from generation to generation. (NLT)

2. **God provides for us as we go through life's seasons.**

 Isaiah 46:4 Even to your old age and gray hairs I am he, I am he who will sustain you. I have made you and I will carry you; I will sustain you and I will rescue you. (NIV)

 Psalm 55:22 Give your burdens to the Lord, and he will take care of you. He will not permit the godly to slip and fall. (NLT)

 Philippians 4:6–7 Do not be anxious about anything, but in every situation, by prayer and petition, with thanksgiving, present your requests to God. And the peace of God, which transcends all understanding, will guard your hearts and your minds in Christ Jesus. (NIV)

Getting through the Emptiness

1. **Patience with each other is essential.**

 1 Corinthians 13:4–5 Love is patient, love is kind. It does not envy, it does not boast, it is not proud. It does not dishonor others, it is not self-seeking, it is not easily angered, it keeps no record of wrongs. (NIV)

 1 Thessalonians 5:14 And we urge you, brothers and sisters, warn those who are idle and disruptive, encourage the disheartened, help the weak, be patient with everyone. (NIV)

 Colossians 3:12–14 Therefore, as God's chosen people, holy and dearly loved, clothe yourselves with compassion, kindness, humility, gentleness and patience. Bear with each other and forgive one another if any of you has a grievance against someone. Forgive as the Lord forgave you. And over all these virtues put on love, which binds them all together in perfect unity. (NIV)

 Ecclesiastes 7:8; Ephesians 4:2–3

2. **Assist your spouse in developing an unselfish biblical attitude concerning your empty nest. Acceptance and contentment are possible through Christ.**

 Philippians 2:3–4 Do nothing from selfishness or empty conceit, but with humility of mind regard one another as more important than yourselves; do not merely look out for your own personal interests, but also for the interests of others. (NASB)

Philippians 4:8 Finally, brothers, whatever is true, whatever is honorable, whatever is just, whatever is pure, whatever is lovely, whatever is commendable, if there is any excellence, if there is anything worthy of praise, think about these things. (ESV)

Philippians 4:11–13 Not that I speak from want, for I have learned to be content in whatever circumstances I am. I know how to get along with humble means, and I also know how to live in prosperity; in any and every circumstance I have learned the secret of being filled and going hungry, both of having abundance and suffering need. I can do all things through Him who strengthens me. (NASB)

3. **Use this time to build a stronger relationship with your spouse.**

Proverbs 21:19 Better to live in a desert than with a quarrelsome and nagging wife. (NIV)

1 Corinthians 7:3–5 The husband should fulfill his wife's sexual needs, and the wife should fulfill her husband's needs. The wife gives authority over her body to her husband, and the husband gives authority over his body to his wife. Do not deprive each other of sexual relations. (NLT)

Proverbs 5:18 May your fountain be blessed, and may you rejoice in the wife of your youth. (NIV)

4. **More opportunity for ministry and service can come with an empty nest. Enrich your world for Christ!**

Psalm 71:18 So even to old age and gray hairs, O God, do not forsake me, until I proclaim your might to another generation, your power to all those to come. (ESV)

Psalm 92:12–14 The righteous flourish like the palm tree and grow like a cedar in Lebanon. They are planted in the house of the Lord; they flourish in the courts of our God. They still bear fruit in old age; they are ever full of sap and green. (ESV)

Titus 2:3–5 Similarly, teach the older women to live in a way that honors God. They must not slander others or be heavy drinkers. Instead, they should teach others what is good. These

> older women must train the younger women to love their husbands and their children, to live wisely and be pure, to work in their homes, to do good, and to be submissive to their husbands. Then they will not bring shame on the word of God. (NLT)

Practical Steps

- Write out your fears/anxieties about children being gone, and research additional Scripture to combat each struggle.
- Your parenting has taken a new focus. Provide encouragement without hovering; plan times to reconnect. Keep lines of communication open; encourage strong marriages. Celebrate new family members—babies, sons-in-law, daughters-in-law.
- Guard against becoming harsh, perfectionistic, opinionated, or controlling. Give advice when asked. Pray daily for your children and their spouses.
- Find new activities you and your spouse can do together.
    - Read a book out loud.
    - Take walks, get a gym membership together.
    - Get a camper, take a vacation, or go on a cruise.
    - Join a couples Bible study.
    - Communicate about joint interests.
    - Go on missions trips. Volunteer at a shelter.
    - Develop interests (painting, writing, cooking, taking classes, mountain climbing) that you wish you could have tried when your house was full.
- If your children have married, pray for their marriages. Encourage them this way, helping them build strong lives together.

Resources

- *Empty Nest* (booklet). Elyse Fitzpatrick. Faith Resources.
- *Sweethearts for a Lifetime*. Wayne Mack. P&R.

- *When You're Facing the Empty Nest.* Mary Ann Froehlich. Bethany House.
- *When Your Children Have Grown . . . It's Time.* Diane Noble. Baker.
- *You Never Stop Being a Parent: Thriving in Relationship with Adult Children.* Elyse Fitzpatrick. P&R.

Further Reference Resources